BRANTFORD PUBLIC LIBRARY
39154900800863

PRAISE FOR *THROW YOUR STI*

D0720323

Throw Your Stuff Off the Plane is a practical guide fc
of self-discovery and will benefit any organizatioi. , ...u in driving
more accountability, this book is for you! But keep a mirror with you at all times and
be ready for some serious self-analysis, as the journey all starts from within.
— Christian Giroux, Area Commercial Director, EMEA,
Abbott Nutrition International, Dubai

I can hear the sound of Art Horn's wise voice as I read *Throw Your Stuff Off the Plane*.
Not only does he get how people are wired, it feels as though he's talking directly to *my*
wiring. And, like a master electrician, he knows how to reposition and tweak it so that I
can be better at life. His book is full of little "aha" moments that explain why we behave
the way we do.
— Elspeth Lynn, Group Creative Director, FCB Inferno, London

Welcome to the world of accountability. In *Throw Your Stuff Off the Plane*, you will find
not only fun personal examples and business ones, but also self-assessment tools to help
you understand where you fit. We all want our teams to nail it, to be highly efficient, to
thrive, but as Art Horn puts it, "that does not preclude the humanistic; it calls for it."
— Jana A. Mihaylova, General Manager, Abbott Nutrition International,
Abbott Laboratories, Fort Bonifacio, Taguig City, Philippines

I don't think I've read a more useful business book in a long time. If you consider
yourself a practitioner of human-centred leadership, you're going to devour this
book. I thought I knew what self-responsibility was before I read this book, but
this exploration of it, and, most importantly, the learning on how to encourage
it in co-workers, is going to be invaluable.
— Andy Macaulay, Managing Partner, Rethink Communications, Toronto

Companies big and small are so focused on getting their people to become
accountable, but they fall short. *Throw Your Stuff Off the Plane* allows us to
delve deeper toward getting our people to become more responsible versus just
accountable. A timely book written by an inspirational leader.
— Hesham Shafie, President and Chief Executive Officer,
Brand Momentum, Toronto

Great book! Ownership, commitment, responsibility, and alignment are qualities we seek for ourselves, those we work and live with, and our organizations. Through insightful discussion and real-life examples, *Throw Your Stuff Off the Plane* clarifies what these qualities look like, how they're interconnected, and how to achieve them.

— Jerry Berman, Area President, M/I Homes, Washington, D.C.

To be accountable or to be a victim is one of those elemental decisions that everyone needs to make. Simply, the former leads you to a happier and more rewarding life. This book is a thoughtful, valuable guide to helping achieve that.

— Rob Pitfield, Chairman, TravelEdge, Toronto

Accountability is what binds high-performance organizations. It is contagious and sets a company up for success. *Throw Your Stuff Off the Plane* is an overdue, straightforward approach to developing a truly accountable and ultimately successful company. This is a must-read for any leader serious about developing and sustaining high-performance teams.

— Tal Bevan, Chief Operating Officer, Architech, Toronto

Art Horn takes readers on a powerful journey to help them identify ways to further empower team members and instill in them the desire to truly take ownership for their work, their results, and the success of the organization.

— Avi Kahn, Chief Executive Officer, Hilti North America, Plano, Texas

Art Horn has done a masterful job of explaining the "art of accountability." Clearly, accountability is the outcome of an organization that values and acts upon commitments, is goal-oriented, and focuses on measureable results that are managed through effective and frequent "coachable moments."

— Paul J. Bognar, Chief Operating Officer/Executive Vice President,
Service Inspired Restaurants, Toronto

What would increase the willingness of individuals to take personal accountability and responsibility for their performance, and what environment would enable this? Art Horn's book offers an insightful look at what individuals can do to be that person and what leaders need to do to facilitate their employees' desire.

— Stephen Girouard, National Sales Director,
Diabetes and Cardiovascular, Sanofi Canada, Montreal

THROW YOUR STUFF OFF THE PLANE

THROW YOUR STUFF OFF THE PLANE

Achieving Accountability in
Business and Life

ART HORN

DUNDURN
TORONTO

Copyright © Art Horn, 2017

All rights reserved. No part of this publication may be reproduced, stored in a retrieval system, or transmitted in any form or by any means, electronic, mechanical, photocopying, recording, or otherwise (except for brief passages for purposes of review) without the prior permission of Dundurn Press. Permission to photocopy should be requested from Access Copyright.

Cover image: istockphoto.com/KazlouskiYury
Printer: Webcom

Library and Archives Canada Cataloguing in Publication

Horn, Arthur H., author

    Throw your stuff off the plane : achieving accountability in business and life / Art Horn.

Includes bibliographical references and index.
Issued in print and electronic formats.
ISBN 978-1-4597-4052-5 (softcover).--ISBN 978-1-4597-4053-2 (PDF).--
ISBN 978-1-4597-4054-9 (EPUB)

    1. Responsibility. 2. Success. 3. Success in business. 4. Self-actualization (Psychology). I. Title.

1 2 3 4 5   21   20 19 18 17

We acknowledge the support of the **Canada Council for the Arts**, which last year invested $153 million to bring the arts to Canadians throughout the country, and the **Ontario Arts Council** for our publishing program. We also acknowledge the financial support of the **Government of Ontario**, through the **Ontario Book Publishing Tax Credit** and the **Ontario Media Development Corporation**, and the **Government of Canada**.

Nous remercions le **Conseil des arts du Canada** de son soutien. L'an dernier, le Conseil a investi 153 millions de dollars pour mettre de l'art dans la vie des Canadiennes et des Canadiens de tout le pays.

Care has been taken to trace the ownership of copyright material used in this book. The author and the publisher welcome any information enabling them to rectify any references or credits in subsequent editions.
— *J. Kirk Howard, President*

The publisher is not responsible for websites or their content unless they are owned by the publisher.

Printed and bound in Canada.

VISIT US AT

 dundurn.com | @dundurnpress | dundurnpress | dundurnpress

Dundurn
3 Church Street, Suite 500
Toronto, Ontario, Canada
M5E 1M2

To all the people who have allowed HORN into their world.

A little nonsense, now and then, is relished by the wisest men.

— Anonymous

CONTENTS

Preface   13

Introduction   17

1   Responsibility   27

2   Accountability   38

3   Commitment   47

4   Willpower   69

5   Free of Blame   82

6   The Twelve Obstacles   100

7   Coaching Yourself   123

8   Being the Boss   139

9   Organizational Accountability   157

Acknowledgements   179

Notes   181

Bibliography   183

Index   185

PREFACE

Thirty-five years ago I made a decision to take a whole new direction in my life. Two weeks later I changed my mind. I was neither accountable to anyone for the decision nor, apparently, even remotely committed to it. A day later I was almost in a plane crash and had to do what the pilot told me to do or we would die. In that case, my accountability wasn't an issue and I was about as committed as one can get.

After 30 years as a leadership consultant, I still find myself informed by the little snippets of insight embedded in such experiences. Feeble decisions, foggy accountabilities, how fear really cranks up one's level of commitment, the nature of commitment born of fear, and what it feels like to have a muscle-tightening, eye-squinting level of determination are all fascinating to me.

The big decision I changed my mind about way back then was to join a cult. I had been seriously involved in the world of meditation and became convinced that joining would put me on a fast track to enlightenment. I had just finished my fourth year of university, and rather than go back to my old summer job in a Northern Ontario logging operation with an eye on graduate school in the autumn, I declared my choice to pack it all in to join a community of like-minded followers of a famed guru.

Two weeks passed. It was the night before the logging operation got started, and I had a bad case of cold feet. My father could barely hide his smile when he heard my explanation. It was as if he knew all along that granting me the freedom to commit my soul would open me to the possibility of not committing my soul, if you know what I mean. His advice was that I call long-distance to the home of the logging company's human resources person to see if I could take the job, even though I had already turned it down.

I made the call. A little boy answered, and he went to get his father on the line. While waiting I told myself that if this guy said it was too late, it would be a message from the universe that I was meant to be a yogi. But he didn't say that.

"Sure, that would be great, but you'll have to be here tomorrow. Can you do that?"

I thought, *Are you kidding? I would jump out of an airplane if that's what it would take.* What I actually said was, "Why, yes, I'm sure I can get there. Thank you very much. Really. Thank you very much!"

I packed a duffle bag with my clothes and loaded up two boxes with my books about meditation, Eastern philosophy, and all the materials from the meditation community I had just left behind. The next morning my father drove me to the airport so I could catch a flight to Thunder Bay, where I would then somehow travel the additional 300 kilometres to the small town of Marathon. I was both relieved and excited.

The exact answer to the question about how I would get to the small town of Marathon came in the men's room at the Thunder Bay airport. Normally I'm not inclined to talk to strangers in a men's room, but I happened to ask the fellow standing next to me if he had any idea how to get to Marathon. "What a coincidence!" he replied. "I'm about to fly right over that area and would be glad to take you there. They have a little landing strip, so it won't be a problem."

Bingo! Fate was unfolding.

The fellow had a little two-seater aircraft. I squeezed my two boxes of books and little duffle bag into a small side door of the plane and hopped into the co-pilot seat, and we taxied out to the runway. The pilot said it was too bad the books were so heavy, but "we should be okay."

During takeoff, he once again mentioned the books. He kept tilting his head and wincing. Over the sound of the engine strain, he raised his voice. "She's a little heavy, but I think we'll be fine."

You *think* we'll be fine? Where's the conviction in that? I had assumed pilots took some sort of chest-thumping responsibility, that there's a lot of accountability built into the system beyond just giving it their best shot. I mean, I wouldn't walk a blind person across the street saying, "There sure are plenty of cars out here, but I think we'll be fine."

It was just 30 seconds later, when we were in the air and I could see the airport buildings shrinking beneath us, that I heard him say, "Oh-oh." He was leaning over and tapping hard on a gauge. I could see panic in his face.

Out the window I saw the huge lake over on the right, dense forest on the left, and that we were already out of town.

The next thing I heard was, "No! We're just too heavy. Throw your stuff off the plane!"

"What?" I asked incredulously over the roar of the engine.

"Throw your stuff off the plane!" He twisted around, quickly pointed at my baggage, and motioned toward the little side door of the plane. "Your stuff — it's too heavy! Throw it out!"

At that particular moment, none of the possible metaphors that now cross my mind dawned on me. And I wasn't about to question a panicking pilot giving a do-it-or-we-crash command.

There is still a part of me that superstitiously believes my spurned guru had a little temper tantrum and with a twirl of his magic wand admonished, "You're either in or you're out, and if you're out, be out. Toss all your pretended wisdom and feigned commitment out the window — now!"

I unbuckled my seat belt and wiggled my way behind the seat, where the two boxes that had absolutely no idea what was about to happen to them were sitting innocently, trembling with the shake of the little airplane. I opened the side hatch of the aircraft and looked down to the ground below and the trees whooshing by. I specifically remember thinking, *This is just bizarre.* I shoved one box out the little door. And then the other.

The sound of the aircraft changed somewhat, and I heard the pilot's relief: "Ahh, that's better." And in seconds it was as if nothing had happened.

I was inclined to answer, *Well, how lovely that you're feeling relieved I pushed my boxes of books off your airplane. How nice I was able to help out like that.*

More directly in touch with my anger toward the pilot, I thought, *Couldn't you have warned me? Couldn't you say, 'Sorry about that'? Or maybe just offer a little explanation with a couple of tokens of remorse?*

I think what I actually said was, "Good." I pretended it was no big deal.

I did have fear about whether we'd actually make it to Marathon. We were, after all, only about one minute into the flight, and already I had thrown out not just my summer reading but also the only tangible connection I had to my dream of the yogic life. I had just tossed it out the window.

All that summer I thought about my boxes of books lying on the forest floor. Up in that area of the country, who knows — they might still be there after 30 years. I never went back to look.

What I look at nowadays are things like how, even if an organization is beautifully designed around accountability, what really makes it hum is a genuine commitment from the people who are being held accountable. I am particularly intrigued by what it feels like to be wholly committed rather than being just a little committed, and intending to do something without any serious commitment rather than having no commitment at all — even when there is accountability.

I think about how time is an enemy of commitment. At one moment, a determined person might declare, "I will exercise daily," and a day later, *poof*, it's as if that person has been replaced with a whole new being. The new guy remembers the former person's intentions but doesn't really share them.

And I think about how mental clutter is another enemy of commitment. Our unresolved feelings, our conflicting obligations, the sheer number of tasks we must juggle — all make for a very heavy load. So some commitments have a better chance of being fulfilled than others.

The amount of determination I brought to shoving my boxes of books off that airplane was way up in the red zone. I could *feel* that intention in my body; it was an eye-squinting, full-blast, *no-matter-what!* kind of willpower. If I had, and sustained, that same level of determination in my commitment to the guru, folks would be calling me Uncle Yogi today.

It still feels good to throw my stuff off the plane. I like the feeling of doing something with all my might.

INTRODUCTION

WEST POINT

Perhaps you've heard that at West Point, the United States Military Academy, first-year students are allowed to say four things — and four things only — to upperclassmen: "Yes, sir," "No, sir," "I do not understand, sir," and, "No excuse, sir."

As you might guess, one reason they have this rule is to keep the young cadets in their place, to make them defer to authority — basically, to tell them who's boss. Particularly in the military, where unquestioned compliance with commands shouted in the battlefield is absolutely critical, subordinates are expected to do what they're told.

At West Point, upperclassmen have been known to ask trick questions of students to test whether the recruits have their heads trained to the principle. For example, an upperclassman stands at Billie's desk, looks down on Billie, and shouts, in a voice as loud and deep as mean drill sergeants can dredge up, the question, "Billie, did you do your homework last night? *Did you do your homework?*"

Billie then might jump to attention and say, quite loudly, because loud and clear is the name of the game, "No, sir!"

And then the trick command: "You tell me why, Billie! You tell me why!"

At this point, Billie feels the impulse to give his explanation. Perhaps it's "The dog ate the book, *sir!*" or "I ran out of time, *sir!*"

It's a human impulse, right? In times of fear, try to please — if the big guy asks a question, answer it. But no; if Billie is smart, he'll answer with,

"No excuse, *sir*!" This would cause Billie to pass the test (and perhaps suffer the consequences related to not completing his homework).

I can't deny I sometimes think it would be nice if the people who were accountable to me would always answer my queries and complaints by simply taking full responsibility. I wouldn't want them to feel the shame and humiliation that goes with that seemingly inhumane treatment, however. No, somehow there has to be a balance between honouring their autonomy and humanity while still getting them to acknowledge that they "own" whatever they touch.

Beyond creating the discipline to "just do what you're told," why does West Point have these rules? They are attempting to form a habit of taking personal responsibility and break the habit of deflecting personal responsibility when things haven't gone according to plan. It's not that there is a lack of realistic explanations for things going wrong; it's that at West Point, the higher priority is to take full personal responsibility for character building. The notion of "I touch it; I own it" isn't a bad line of thinking to adopt.

Let's say you're late for a meeting because, in fact, your previous meeting ended late and it was important. You get to the next meeting and say to the folks in the room, "Sorry I'm late, everybody. My last meeting ran over." Bingo. That's you deflecting the responsibility away from yourself and over to things seemingly out of your control. That's the habit West Point is trying to break. At West Point, someone senior to you would pull you aside, look you square in the eyes, and, with a raised voice, yell something like, "No excuses! That meeting wasn't the issue. Your planning was the issue." Or "Your inability to assert yourself was the issue." Or "Your inability to influence people to excuse you so you could live by your word was the issue." Or "Your lack of personal organization around rearranging *this* meeting was the issue. It was *you*. It was *not* that *last meeting*. Grow up!" The general principle is that making excuses is pathetic. Whatever happened, you should have seen it coming. Whatever limitations you face, you should have overcome them. Spending people's time on your defence is insulting.

> When we leap to explanations rather than shine the light on what might have been our failure, we bypass our responsibility.

Indeed, reasons are things we learn from so that we can eliminate problems in the future, and there is a time and place to consider them. But when we leap to explanations rather than shine the light on what might have been our failure, we bypass our responsibility; if we had the habit of taking full responsibility in the first place, we might have avoided our problems. We'll explore responsibility in more detail in Chapter 1.

ACCOUNTABILITY

As we'll see in Chapter 2, people use the word *accountability* to highlight that if you don't come through, you're going to have to account for it, as Ricky Ricardo admonishes Lucy in the old *I Love Lucy* television series. With his Cuban accent and Latin style, he'd say, "All right, start 'splainin'!" Of course, people would rather not need an explanation from the people they're frustrated with — they would rather avoid the problem in the first place — but getting someone to account for performance is like a fallback. "You failed me. Now explain!"

> The notion of accountability has emerged as a human tool to motivate people — do what you're supposed to do or you'll be held to account.

We might say the notion of accountability has emerged as a human tool to motivate people — do what you're supposed to do or you'll be held to account. The impulse to get people to be accountable is revealed when you're on the phone with a customer service agent dealing with some mess or other: the person tells you what he or she is going to do to move your situation along, and you ask the agent for his or her name. You're somehow elevating the probability of success by implying that if they don't do what they said, then, darn it, you'll tell on them!

The impulse also shows up when you're sitting in a meeting and the boss asks, "Who's going to handle this particular task?" You raise your hand, say, "I'll do it," and make yourself accountable. You publicly put yourself out there, with skin in the game, as if you're saying, "You can chase me down, admonish me, and perhaps even punish me in some, hopefully small, way if I don't do this to a modicum of satisfaction."

Organizations depend on accountability so they can accomplish their results. If it weren't for coordinated task lists and feedback systems that allow management to hold people accountable, things just would *not* go swimmingly at all. Chaos would ensue. Accordingly, organizations often make a mission out of ratcheting up the level of accountability in their ranks. They usually take a healthy, *systemic* approach derived from accepted performance management protocols:

- Clarify organizational and individual objectives.
- Ensure job responsibilities are clearly defined.
- Measure performance against established standards.
- Educate.
- Improve processes.
- Ensure communication systems are in place that will pre-empt crises.
- Tie compensation to achieving and exceeding expectations.
- Elevate inter- and intra-departmental co-operation by creating a shared understanding of roles.
- Make sure the "consequences" of failure are clear.

The problem is that, well, people are people. Despite all the systems in place to ensure accountability, you just can't control people. It's the old free-will problem, combined with the allure of the common vices known to all of us. For heaven's sake, we can't even control ourselves, let alone our organizations!

My wife made cupcakes one day. I'm trying to watch my sugar intake, so I allowed myself one cupcake after dinner. My wife left the room. Five minutes later, I admit, I was ramming another sugary cupcake into my face just as my wife was walking back into the room. I got caught.

Indeed, people make promises to themselves and others, and then break them with surprising ease. Chapter 3 will focus specifically on what we can do to make commitments that stick, and in Chapter 4 we'll look at the mechanics of willpower with an eye to bolstering our self-control.

By way of summary, West Point has rules that say, "Don't even think about explaining why you didn't come through." Other organizations have systems in place to compensate for the natural human tendency to eat meta-phoric cupcakes, and individuals have the promises they make to themselves — but, by gosh, things get in the way.

This book is about some powerful tools that you and your organization can add to your tool box in order to counter the momentum of organizational free-for-all.

BECOMING MORE "RESPONSIBLE"

Our bottom line in this book is this: if you want someone to be more account-able, help that person become more responsible. That means getting the per-son to feel genuinely committed, to take ownership, to experience willpower.

When people become more "responsible," the organization to which they belong has fewer accountability problems. That's because being respon-sible implies that one does what one *ought* to do — there is less need for systems of accountability. This is not to say that I know what the "right thing" is; it's only that I believe responsible people aspire to do it. Even by definition, when we say, "It was the responsible thing to do," we're saying, "It was the right thing to do."

> When people become more responsible there is less need for accountability.

The idea is that the best way to get someone to be accountable (to the team, the boss, the organization as a whole) is to get the person to become a more responsible person — not because they will undertake an assignment knowing there will be trouble if activities aren't undertaken or goals aren't achieved, but because he or she is more likely to do what we all know responsible people tend to do:

- the right thing;
- what they say they will do;
- the things that are called for in the situation; and
- things that are aligned with their values.

BEING SELF-RESPONSIBLE VERSUS BEING RESPONSIBLE IN THE WORLD

We are going to subdivide in this book the notion of "being responsible" into two different areas: being self-responsible and being responsible in the world. Both are good things. They just happen to come from different realms of consideration. One is about oneself, as in, "I behave responsibly concern-ing my well-being." The other — being responsible in the world — is about oneself in the context of one's job, relationships, and society in general.

Lots of people are responsible, but they don't exhibit a lot of self-responsibility. On the other hand, some people aren't what we would call responsible, but they take great care of themselves. We are looking for both. Of course, everyone is self-responsible to some extent already, and I mean that in two ways. First, you couldn't really survive in this world if you didn't actually take some degree of personal responsibility for how things turn out. If you're thirsty, for example, surely you get yourself something to drink. Second, of course, you're responsible! It's your body, your mind, your *being*, no matter how you slice and dice it. What are you going to do with it? Who else *could be* responsible for what *you* choose to do with *your* body?

Finding more self-responsibility and becoming more responsible in the world means aligning what you say and do with what you think and feel, making genuine commitments, and owning your outcomes.

The mandate to act responsibly towards ourselves as individuals and towards all others presents us with the seemingly never ending quest to determine who failed whom when things don't go so well. This propensity will be explored in Chapter 5, "Free of Blame." It will be an invitation to rise above the daily interpretations we make about our lives.

Ultimately, finding more self-responsibility and becoming more responsible in the world means clearing out the cobwebs in your own head: acknowledging the tricks your mind plays on you and learning to sidestep them if you feel they hold you back, getting in touch with the feeling of ownership, aligning what you say and do with what you think and feel, making genuine commitments, getting past blame, and owning your outcomes.

PROBLEMS WITH RESPONSIBILITY

In Chapters 6 and 7 of this book, we get down to brass tacks. What obstacles hold us back from being a responsible person? What can we do to become an even more responsible person? And what can we do for others?

All of us have parts of our lives in which we let ourselves down. For one thing, there are more "shoulds" for us to address than it's humanly possible to fulfill. By nature our minds typically run a behind-the-scenes, automatic program that constantly evaluates whether what we are observing matches our sense of how it ought to be. For most of us, the gap is significant and appears frequently, such that we have an unending flow of "should" experiences popping in the popcorn maker of our heads. Of course, we operate on the assumption that many of the "shoulds" apply to other people (for instance, "My boss should clean up his act"), but depending on how we tend to interpret things, we assign our fair share of "shoulds" to ourselves (for instance, "I should be talking to him about that" or "I should be there for my mother").

Usually, these matters are a bit of a secret for us. Why would I want to admit that I'm afraid of rejection, or reluctant to confront, or guilty of this, or angry about that, or in over my head? In a strange way, we even keep some of these assessments secret from ourselves. Or at least they pop up so quickly we don't have time to reflect. They're just under the surface; you might even call them preverbal. But if we give a voice to our sense of the specific matter, we find ourselves thinking or saying things like, "I know I should …" It could be about anything: how you're raising your kids; whether you work hard enough; how much alcohol you drink; that you should exercise more; confront a certain person; face certain facts; reveal the truth about a certain thing. The list is about as long as there are people on the planet, particularly because most of us have several such "deficiencies."

For what it's worth, I encourage you to make no change unless you want to. This isn't a book about how you ought to become superwoman or superman. This is a book that will help you in the areas you feel ready to tackle more responsibly, and if you're a leader, it will help you to get the people on your team to embrace more ownership on the job (to the extent they're open to it).

The good news is that the obstacles to being more responsible are finite in number, and we're going to explore several of the most common and look at examples of how people with those impediments in their thinking managed to get around them. We'll see how sometimes simply shining a light on the problem, increasing our basic understanding of unconscious dynamics in our thinking, will tend to diffuse or defuse the hidden "should" and enable greater responsibility to emerge.

Let's take a very simple example. A woman named Susan admitted to herself (and me) that she would like to prospect for new business more than she does. Susan has an account role in a communications and public-relations business — basically bringing in revenue for her company. Susan's time is usually invested on accounts that have been doing business with her firm for years. However, lately there has been a push to get new clients. This will require Susan to network with her large circle of business and personal relationships to create business opportunities. Susan isn't a fan of prospecting. But she admits that the "responsible thing" would be to make a habit out of regularly reaching out and attempting to book meetings to discuss her company's services — "responsible" not just in the eyes of her employer because she's actually agreed to do it, but also responsible to herself. She feels she's somehow letting herself down.

I asked Susan to tell me more about what was holding her back from getting started. She said, "I don't know. It's something about it suddenly changing the relationship from being easygoing, based on no self-interest, to being, 'Oh, here's Susan using me. I can't trust Susan anymore.'"

"How so?" I asked.

"Well, nobody on my list sees me as selling to them. They assume I'm just me. There's no ulterior motive. Do you know what I mean? I think it would be pretty awkward to just start asking them which of their personal contacts I can approach. They wouldn't know whether I was being friendly because I'm friendly or being friendly just to get what I want. Everyone knows I'm in sales, but they don't think my selfish motives invade our relationship. Now, from their perspective, I might secretly be *using* them."

This was a great example of a "should" experience caused by what she knew she was expected to do versus what she was currently comfortable doing. Susan was blocked.

I asked her if she felt proud of the quality of her company's work, and she answered that yes, her firm has consistently changed the course of its client organizations for the better. I also asked her if she trusted herself to be friendly and genuine, even when she wanted to move someone in some way (for instance, to get the name of someone to contact). She was positive about that, too, highlighting that her concern was about what the other person might be thinking — not about whether her personal behaviour would change.

I put this question to her: "So, how could you approach people, keeping in mind your confidence in both the quality of your firm's work and your own ability to just be straight and friendly with people, in a way that wouldn't make them feel funny about your motives?"

Her answer was quick and clear, as though it were already waiting there just behind a doorway. "I could say that I've taken on the mission of generating new client relationships and would like to know if they'd be willing to help me make connections with firms that might have a tangible need to do what my firm does."

"And would you be able to do it in a relaxed fashion?"

"I doubt it; not initially, anyway."

We agreed that practice — not role playing, but asking people she knew would be supportive — would make a big difference. Over the subsequent weeks, Susan proceeded as she described, and a month or so later she successfully closed new business with new clients.

I hope you noticed that I didn't actually give Susan any advice. All I did was allow her to say out loud what was holding her back and to ask her what was possible within her comfort range. We just talked it through. This is a key point. Many of the things that hold us back from acting the way we wish we would act are simple, unconscious methods our brains use to, essentially, put things off. By shining a light on the little mental obstacle and exploring it, sometimes only a bit, we move right through it.

> Many of the things that hold us back from acting the way we "should" are simple, unconscious methods our brains use to, essentially, put things off.

Of course, at other times the block is bigger. If Susan had been dealing with a deep fear of rejection, for example, there would probably have been more work involved. Or if she wasn't prospecting because she was at some level punishing her employer for *making* her prospect, that, too, would have been tougher. If she were holding a secret about potentially leaving her employer for another communications firm, yes, that would be a quandary, but likely still resolvable by unpacking it and making some choices.

ORGANIZATIONAL ACCOUNTABILITY

Let's say that Susan never engaged in the above discussion with me, nor had she thought it through independently, and simply continued procrastinating vis-à-vis prospecting for new business. Perhaps her employer, uncovering that Susan had indeed brought no new accounts in for a period of several months, had an internal meeting among the firm's partners.

One partner says to another, "Look at Susan, for example. She hasn't done anything when it comes to prospecting! You know what? We have an accountability problem around here and it's like the elephant in the room. We all know it. People agree to do things, they never do them, and we let them get away with it. We need to get out of this rut."

Interestingly, they, too, might be hiding from themselves regarding addressing their accountability problem. One person shone a light on the problem, maybe one or two others nodded affirmation, but the conversation is easily steered by an innocent-seeming effort to build on the idea. One partner pipes up, "We need to make bringing in new business a condition of employment!" Another partner jumps in and says, "We should track the number of appointments each account person sets up with new companies and put together some kind of contest to reward the person who has the most first appointments per quarter!"

With this conversational momentum, they feel as if they're honouring the comment about the accountability problem, but they move on before nailing it down. Too bad. It just goes to show that organizational account-ability is one full order of magnitude more complex than self-accountability. Nonetheless, they have begun to explore a few systemic tweaks.

In Chapter 8, we'll begin to explore some basic principles leaders can leverage to optimize the amount of personal responsibility people take in their organization. But we'll end this introduction, and later the book in Chapter 9, with the argument that the systemic elements usually installed to optimize accountability aren't sufficient to achieve their desired effects. What's critical is the ability of leaders to be graceful as they balance their desire to control with their need to enable.

1
RESPONSIBILITY

In my experience, when someone complains about an "accountability problem" in their organization, they are thinking of at least one of four things:

- a lack of ownership felt among team members
- failures not being addressed
- rampant blame and finger pointing
- recurring problem avoidance

The solutions to the accountability dilemmas tend to fall into two categories: systemic changes (to things like job descriptions, operational procedures, and organizational structure); and soft, less tangible, people-based interventions. The latter category can be called attitudinal, as in, pertaining to the attitudes people have toward their own responsibilities and responsibility in general. The attitudinal approach to the solution is the subject of this book. That solution usually calls for a journey in self-awareness on the part of the people involved. We'll take that journey together, starting with exploring the ideas of responsibility and accountability.

Commitment and willpower are natural elements of the journey, because they go hand in hand with finding and retaining feelings of ownership. Also natural is the temptation to resist ownership and blame others, so we shall blame *blame*, if you will, for a brief while.

The journey isn't just for the people around us; it's for each of us. Indeed, all of us could surely do with a reminder of what it means, for example, to take good care of ourselves. So let's start with a look at the very basic idea of being responsible.

BEING RESPONSIBLE

I asked a 90-year-old woman whom I consider wise what she thought it meant to be a responsible person, and she said that responsible people do things such as keep their promises, tell the truth, pay their taxes, vote, and put out of its misery a suffering animal they might have run across (don't ask). In other words, she cited examples of responsible behaviour, and I agreed that her examples seemed to poke at something juicy.

I also asked a nine-year-old boy whom I consider to be precocious what he thought it meant to be a responsible person, and he said it meant you can't just do what you want. That pretty much summed up things for me, too. Responsibility seems to be about something bigger than the individual.

Personally, I think *being responsible* relates to behaving in a way that benefits or supports something bigger than what we currently are — maybe it supports our organization, our relationships, our family, our nation, our planet, our future. For example, responsible people don't litter, and by resisting the temptation to litter, they protect something bigger than themselves. Responsible people pay their debts and, in so doing, support their relationships and strengthen our economic system. A responsible driver obeys the rules of the road and, in so doing, helps maintain some semblance of system-wide traffic order. Generally, a responsible person is someone we can trust.

For clarity, I'm not saying that taking on more responsibility makes one a more responsible person. (Even though those who take on bigger roles in their organizations might be said to be more responsible, let's not assume that makes them more responsible persons.) No. When we use the label *responsible person*, we're referring to the personal attribute of *being responsible*, in the way people talk about, for example, a good babysitter. Of course, a major premise in this book is that increasing the level of accountability in an organization means getting everybody into hyper-good-babysitter mode — people who align themselves with the point of the situation but who can think independently; rational people who work pretty hard but can still be playful. Babysitters need to be playful!

HAVING RESPONSIBILITY

We've talked about being responsible, but not about the *idea* of responsibility or what a responsibility actually is and where it comes from (other than just being assigned). Basically, responsible people address their responsibilities head-on. But all of us wrestle with some responsibilities more than others. Indeed, sometimes responsibility is like a hot potato that somebody tosses you. It is hot to the touch, so if you're lucky, you can quickly toss it to someone else — *you* don't want it. Sometimes, though, when someone such as a boss tosses us a responsibility, we have to hold on to it, and we begrudgingly say, "Okay." That's when it's possible to have a responsibility but not be committed to it. Wonder where accountability problems come from? Right there — when people catch or must fulfill responsibilities that for one reason or another they don't embrace.

Let's look at a personal example. On the list of my duties in my household is the weekly job of taking out the garbage. Occasionally, I forget — garbage day is always the same day of the week, but sometimes I wake up forgetting to ask myself, "Is this that day?"

When my wife points out that I missed a garbage day, there's usually a little discussion about it. She'll say, "You forgot to take the garbage out again."

I'll respond with, "Darn. Sorry about that."

Her inevitable reply is, "You aren't sorry enough to remember consistently."

What we have here is a duty to be done and a relatively lightweight attitude toward that duty. In terms of the responsibility one has to oneself to own the tasks one takes on, we could say, at least in this realm of household responsibilities, that I reveal a pretty lame level of responsibility. I'm fairly committed, but not wholly committed. I'm accountable for it — insofar as someone can expect me to account for a failure to fulfill the duty — but I wouldn't say I have a genuine sense of personal accountability, at least around this particular household matter.

> Wonder where accountability problems come from? They arise when people must fulfill responsibilities they don't embrace.

SOCIAL RESPONSIBILITIES

We let ourselves off the hook for little lapses in responsibility, but we readily judge others regarding whether they're fulfilling their social responsibilities for fair behaviour:

- It's not fair of you to leave your coffee cup in the sink at the office for someone else to clean up.
- It's not fair for you to sneak out while teammates are working hard on the team's behalf.
- It's not fair to ignore the rules of the road.
- It's not fair to cut in line rather than wait your turn.
- It's not fair to remove goods from the store without paying for them.

Corporate responsibility works the same way. A company has a responsibility to provide value for money — products that are worth what people have to pay for them. Otherwise, it's not fair. You can't sell spoiled food. You can't mess up the chemicals that go into prescription drugs. You can't spend less on safety standards and thereby put the health of employees in jeopardy — because it's not fair. Corporations have a responsibility to be fair.

But one could ask, "Who's to say we have a responsibility to be fair? If I don't *feel* this compunction, where does it come from? How does it follow?" Great questions. Nobody knows.

One seventeenth-century view, that of Thomas Hobbes in his philosophical work *Leviathan*, is that there is an unspoken agreement among all people that we'll be fair with one another, lest we act on greed, lust, envy, and all the other deadly sins; have one heck of a drunken brawl; and, as one would expect in slippery-slope conditions, basically kill one another off.

> Perhaps the compunction to be responsible can be traced to the basic human desire to feel whole or connected to something bigger.

Another view is that through natural selection our gene pool has favoured the ability to put ourselves in someone else's shoes. Knowing how we would feel and judge if we observed certain behaviour in someone else, we can speculate how others might feel if they observe that behaviour in us — we self-manage accordingly. Similarly, being born with the ability to feel what others are feeling makes compassion possible. Perhaps our sense of responsibility comes from wanting to invest ourselves in the people and entities we care about.

Needless to say, our values and behaviours are heavily influenced by our family, education, friendships, religious affiliations, and the media. They, too, could be the source of the responsibility sense.

My favourite view is that the compunction to be responsible can be traced to the basic human desire to feel whole or connected to something bigger. From the dawn of our personal sense of self, this craving has driven us to reconcile the competing motivations inside us while accommodating the complexities of our relationships with others and life at large. What emerges is a growing clarity that the universe offers us a carrot: if you want to get to the target (wholeness), you have to co-operate with others and you have to be responsible. We align ourselves with this universal algorithm, and our personal evolution yields progressively more responsible behaviour.

> The extent of an organization's culture of accountability is partly a function of individuals operating from a place where they *actually feel* responsible.

Notwithstanding the possible validity of these explanations for the impulse to be responsible for something, the important point here is that the extent of an organization's culture of accountability is partly a function of individuals operating from a place where they actually feel responsible.

OWNERSHIP

Let's face it, there can be great joys involved in having a responsibility — like the joy of being a parent or the gratification of being granted authority to make and act on decisions — but there is also the onus of ownership. If you accept a task, you *own* it and carry that responsibility with you until it's done. Some of us walk around sweating like hikers weighed down by huge backpacks, while others stroll gaily through life with little handbags of light-weight duties. Either way, we carry them or we drop them.

Some people take their responsibilities — even their responsibility to themselves — very seriously. They *feel* a sense of ownership for the job they've taken on, the commitments they've made, the issues that have crossed their path, fairness, and compassion toward the planet, other people, and themselves. However, most people participate in what I would call a "partial ownership" scheme of responsibility management regarding their duties on the job, as well as their duties to themselves and others in their private lives. But that's okay. This book isn't about getting everyone to fully own everything they touch; it's meant to help you if you want to own more.

And it's meant to help you help others to own more if they want to or if you can responsibly convince them it's in their best interest to do so.

Someone once admitted to me that she thought herself to be a "half-miler" in her approach to her job. She wasn't really interested in working hard, because her thoughts and dreams were about her kids and their future. The main obstacle to full ownership, as she put it, was that she was fatigued every day because, as a single mother juggling her son back and forth between babysitters, her ex-husband, her in-laws, school, and the various extra-care services she had to take advantage of, she just didn't have the bandwidth to be highly responsible at work. She also resented how she was treated by her colleagues, who saw her as the person who did everything they didn't want to do, and who only partly explained their expectations and got angry with her no matter how well she performed.

This woman works in an organization that's on a mission to increase accountability. Would its analysis of root cause uncover anything more than that she's part of an unhappy work community? Her company operates on the assumption that people complain about her and that she's an example of a low-accountability person (because she allegedly doesn't own up to things she's involved in that go wrong). She admits to herself and she admitted to me that she doesn't feel a sense of ownership! What should her firm do?

Well, systemically it should make roles and responsibilities clear so that people know what they can ask her to accomplish for them. The company might want to ensure she's aware of her contribution to the big picture. It might even consider ensuring her compensation plan and her job description are aligned with her goals and needs.

I would suggest going one step deeper: the organization should also engage her supervisor to get to know her more. Without having to become a counsellor or therapist, that boss could use dialogue to uncover what motivates this employee and how the organization could shape her duties and work responsibilities around her life situation and aspirations. The supervisor could talk about the idea of her gracefully pushing back when she feels taken advantage of. He or she could support the employee's self-esteem by giving her genuinely challenging tasks that, when fulfilled, would justify greater self-respect. Their conversations could, interspersed conveniently over weeks and months, gradually move her to greater job ownership. This, I propose, is what great one-on-one leadership looks like.

It's the stuff of inspiring ownership and self-responsibility. We'll talk about these kinds of dialogues in Chapters 8 and 9.

THE FEELING OF OWNERSHIP

I don't know about you, but I used to love the first day of school. It was the proverbial clean-slate situation: new clothes, new pencil case, fresh commitment, and positive attitude. There were no responsibilities yet, of course — nothing in particular to be accomplished, no impending due dates or tests coming up. It was a present-moment kind of thing. Essentially, just show up. And definitely, if you had asked me, "Arthur, do you own this mission of doing a great job in school this year? Do you take full responsibility for your success?" you can be sure I would have answered with a resounding affirmative, "Absolutely!" And this wouldn't just be a child's go-with-the-flow reply; it would reflect a genuine feeling of readiness to do the work and do really, really well. No responsibilities yet, but a full-fledged feeling of "bring it on" just the same.

Same goes for jobs. I think people show up for a new job with a similar clean slate, fully intending to please, do good work, and be productive. Committed and ready to behave responsibly. In this day-one way, we experience the clean slate of ownership, fully intending to be both self-responsible and responsible for what we touch. I think it's a natural, optimistic state. When we aren't burdened by the day-to-day challenges of our situation, we get in touch with a raw, simple feeling of ownership. And out of our hope, our optimism, we invest ourselves.

> People show up for a new job with a clean slate, fully intending to please, do good work, and be productive. Committed and ready to behave responsibly.

You own you. You are the cause agent, the individual who makes things happen, the decider of all things "you." In the context of your circumstances, whatever they are, however gloomy they might appear to be on other days, you're the one who sets the next step in motion.

Most of us don't quite stick to this clean-slate feeling of ownership. Other feelings can bleed into our psyche. On a bad day, for example, the challenges in front of us can be daunting, such that rather than feeling empowered, we feel overloaded. Or when a task we've taken on goes sour, perhaps we feel shame or guilt or anger. In these cases, somewhere in our emotional makeup there are tangles, obstacles to our sense of being the agent in charge. Chapters 6 and 7 will explore how we can unravel those tangles.

SELF-RESPONSIBILITY

A whole other angle on responsibility is the extent to which people can actually trust themselves to take care of themselves and to make space to self-actualize.

And for many people, that's the hardest thing of all.

A colleague of mine, for example, will readily say, "Yes, sure, I'll take that on," and practically work himself to the point of exhaustion in the process of fulfilling the task. He might appear to an outsider peering in to be very responsible, but he might be failing at *self*-responsibility, so the accurate descriptor of his status might net out at "fairly responsible."

> In some senses, I equate being self-responsible with taking care of oneself, managing one's future, and personal integrity.

In some senses, I equate being self-responsible with taking care of oneself, managing one's future, and personal integrity. The last element, a part of self-responsibility, involves being able to look at yourself in the mirror and say:

- I live by my values.
- I own my consequences.
- I am my word.
- I try my best.
- I seek to self-understand.
- I try to be authentic in my relations with others.
- I am open to hearing where I slip up, and I own my slip-ups.
- I can look inside myself and genuinely report, "I'm trying, I'm trying."
- I honour myself.

I believe the above elements of self-responsibility *join* the list of what's necessary for the genuinely accountable organization. That is, the organization needs people who are both self-responsible *and* responsible in the world, as depicted in the graphic below. Notice how being a responsible person comprises five traits altogether: self-nurturing, effectively managing the day-to-day and one's own future, having personal integrity and being

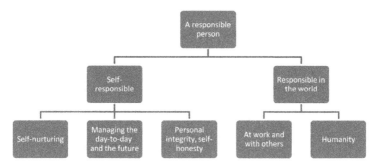

Figure 1: A responsible person is both self-responsible and responsible in the world.

honest with one's self, being responsible at work and with others, and being responsible toward humanity as a whole.

But nurturing the two main types of responsibility isn't often what organizations do when they attempt to increase their level of accountability. Instead, they initiate a root-cause analysis — scanning systems, communications, and even the attitudes of the people (but not quite down to the outlook of unique individuals) — and they direct their attention to the usual suspects: unclear objectives, control problems, the absence of consequences — maybe even poor morale. Their response is to ensure that

- there is clarity of vision, mission, and objectives;
- there are clear lines of responsibility regarding who does what;
- all people understand their contributions to overall performance;
- people "sign off" on, or give their personal commitments to, their objectives;
- feedback loops exist so that matters are addressed before problems happen;
- there are written statements of consequences for failed performance;
- compensation plans are aligned with targeted behaviours and outcomes; and
- poor performers are exited from the organization.

Of course, all of the above help, and a book about how to execute each of them gracefully could be written. But this book is about a different and, in my experience, necessary ingredient in the accountability recipe that's absent from the above list. It's the secret sauce: getting the individuals who make up the organization to find and nurture greater responsibility within themselves. These responsible individuals manifest this disposition by fully addressing their larger purpose and by honouring themselves.

RESPONSIBILITY SELF-ASSESSMENT

We're assuming, of course, that work groups find synergy and produce optimally when people behave responsibly (from their point of view). But let's address *you* for a few moments. How would you assess your own level of responsibility?

Score yourself from 1 to 5 for each item in the following survey. A 5 means you feel very strongly that this trait describes you. A 1 means you're very clear that the trait is a problem for you. As you might guess, a 3 is the basic "more or less." Answer in the context of your professional life.

1. Do you seek to clarify what you're responsible for and, until it's clarified, assume it's your responsibility to fix things that might go wrong? ☐
2. Do you demonstrate a "can-do," "I own it" sense of commitment to your job, its tasks, and the little things that cross your path? ☐
3. Do you only commit to things you can realistically be expected to do? (Challenging but realistic goals are good; unrealistic goals aren't.) ☐
4. Do you do what you say you're going to do, or, if you can't, then pre-emptively manage the expectations of others so they aren't surprised by unmet deadlines or seeing less than they were expecting? ☐
5. Do you demonstrate a genuine willingness to be held accountable by others for failure? ☐
6. Do you apologize and seek to repair when you botch things up? ☐
7. Do you openly, calmly, non-judgmentally, firmly, and persistently deal with others who have let you down? ☐

8. Do you self-accept your failures or limitations? ☐

9. Do you employ systems or tools to help you stay on top of what must get done? ☐

10. Do you deliberately find ways to balance your life so that you demonstrate to yourself that you care for yourself? ☐

11. Do you aspire to authenticity such that you try to be honest with people as much as you possibly can? ☐

12. Do you contribute in some way to society or to the planet (for example, vote, actively recycle, or give to charity)? ☐

TOTAL: _____

Interestingly, most people tend to score themselves higher on responsibility than others score them (unless they happen to be people who are particularly hard on themselves, in which case the opposite is true). That's because of a natural bias. In fact, it might be fun to assess yourself and a couple of other people using the same survey items. When I've facilitated discussions with small groups of people who approached the survey in this way, they've consistently discovered their natural biases in their self-assessments. And because of the feedback from others, they usually get a bit more realistic about themselves.

In terms of your score, assume two things: if the total of your scores was 40 or higher, you're a pretty responsible person. If it was under 25, you have several areas for productive self-reflection. Actually, each of us could pick our lowest-scoring answers and reflect on what we could do to become more self-responsible.

Now, I've never met anyone who embodies all of the above traits all of the time, but I assume we agree when it comes to how to approach relationships and work in team- and goal-oriented environments — those are virtues to which we all aspire. They're traits leaders seek in order to inspire within the communities they lead. In Chapter 7, "Coaching Yourself," we'll revisit this topic with a similar but more rigorous survey — one that specifically differentiates being responsible in the world from being self-responsible, but we have plenty of ground to cover on the path between.

2
ACCOUNTABILITY

THE FEELING OF ACCOUNTABILITY

When I was a teenager, I smoked cigarettes. Each time I would buy a new pack I'd undertake a series of routine hand motions: rip off the plastic wrap that surrounded the package and toss that wrapper either onto the ground or in some other conspicuous place; flip open the cardboard lid, peel off the foil that covered the 20 soldier-like fellas standing at attention, and toss that, too; whip out a smoke; and light it up. I think I got some sort of pleasure from this sequence of activities — not only because the motion was positively reinforced by the squinty-eyed first drag of a fresh cigarette out of a sealed pack of smokes, but also because I was perhaps seen as a cool cigarette smoker with smooth digital dexterity.

Anyway, after a few years of that phase, I became more self-conscious about the judgments others might make about my wantonly tossing refuse onto the ground. This social self-consciousness is one element of the psychology of accountability. It points to the fear of being seen. At times the fear is about being judged unfavourably. At other times, or for some people, the issue is one of merely being seen at all; sometimes we don't want to be seen.

The feeling of accountability is different from the feeling of ownership we talked about at the end of the previous chapter. That was about a sense of power or personal authority over oneself. But this particular feeling is more like a fear — in the case of my being seen as "one who litters," a fear of being judged. But it can also be a fear of just getting into trouble. It's even possible to feel accountable through a fear of how you feel about yourself! For example, you could be walking around the planet carrying a sense of shame, believing that you're a bad person. You probably have an idea of how you ought to behave, so your fear that you won't live up to that — and will, therefore, fulfill your belief that you're a bad person — creates a feeling of accountability. This accountability translates into personally responsible behaviour (although not in an exciting way that allows you to express personal empowerment).

This isn't to say that the feeling of accountability has to be experienced as a negative. It could also be felt as a hopeful opportunity to be seen favourably by others. If you assign me a task that I enjoy doing well, and you mention you'll check in with me a little later, then I might carry extra enthusiasm as I approach the task, anticipating your approbation.

In its healthiest form, a culture of accountability implies that people know they might have to think through and describe to others what went wrong, but they don't do it out of fear; they do it because that's what being responsible is about. They trust that the team is focused on getting things right, not on who is to blame. They know that the mission is to work toward a more productive future, and they're busy trying to discover how that can be accomplished. There is no threat; there is just opportunity. There is no blame; there is merely the need for increased communication.

SIMPLY RATIONAL

Indeed, we create accountability in others when we indicate there will be some future check-in on something or a simple regrouping to see how things are going. The accountability setter (for example, a leader or teammate) might not have any emotional baggage regarding the check-in, and the person who takes on a responsibility might not have any emotions, such as fear or craving, about being seen.

"Okay, I'll see you back here at three and we'll see how it goes." Depending on the context of that remark, such expectation-setting might be efficient. Or it might make you think, "He doesn't trust me!" Or "Good. I'll be better prepared this time." Or "Whooaahh, I'll knock this out of the park, and that's when I'll ask for my raise!"

Accountability is about the possibility of explaining yourself. Sure, there might be not-so-hot consequences for a failure to meet expectations, or maybe wonderful outcomes from the successful fulfillment of those expectations, but in and of themselves, accountabilities are innocent. They're simply rational. We need to know and agree on who's doing what when. If your company wants you to keep track of your activity, yes, it makes you accountable, but it doesn't have to provoke. That's up to your interpretation and the context of your environment.

Accountability is about the possibility of explaining yourself.

But accountability becomes much more provocative when things go awry. And it becomes super-provocative when things go awry regularly and nobody seems to do anything about it. Let's look at a couple of juicy examples.

A LINE IN THE SAND

I was at a client's board meeting recently where six wise old gentlemen were sitting in a fancy mahogany-panelled boardroom, giving a hard time to the CEO of the organization. I was only present to participate in a discussion about a matter later on the agenda, but my presence wasn't an obstacle to open dialogue. I had attended this company's board meetings before.

This part of the meeting was about recent poor financial performance. Sales volume was down, expenses were up, and, of course, profit was terrible. Quite legitimately, the board members were aggressively trying to get to the bottom of the poor performance. They were holding the CEO accountable.

The chairman of the board leaned forward in his swivel chair and said to the CEO, "Look, it's pretty obvious you have an accountability problem. These numbers are pathetic and you know it. You have a reputation for not holding people accountable, and it's directly affecting shareholder value. We want to know the cause of this mess, and I want to know what you're doing about it. I think you let people get away with things, and I don't see any signs otherwise. I never hear of you firing anyone. I'm sorry to be so direct about this, but somebody has to be direct around here. Are you afraid to confront your people?"

The CEO was flustered. You could see it in his face and posture. A bead of perspiration shone on his forehead. From my angle, I could see his leg bouncing up and down as he processed what he was hearing and assembled ideas for a response. The eyes of everyone in the room shifted back and forth from the chairman to the CEO. This was the showdown moment.

Having seen this kind of situation before, not just at the board level but also up and down the ranks of organizations, I knew the people at the top of the hierarchy wanted to hear that an aggressive response was already in motion. They tend to particularly like it when they hear that at least somebody is being, or already has been, dismissed. And certainly they want a plan.

Now, I happen to know this CEO fairly well. He was very familiar with exactly what went wrong over the last financial reporting period, in terms of a strained marketplace and internal problems processing orders, and he knew all along that operating expenses were going to see a tangible but temporary bounce. His private belief was that, in the mid-term, things would likely improve quite a bit because of internal problem-solving efforts already performed.

I also happen to know that he's a softie — not particularly inclined to confront people. The chairman was right about that. The upside to the CEO's style is that people adore him and stay with him, and the downside is that when performance numbers are suffering, other people blame his weak leadership. He knows he has a fear of confrontation. He is trying to improve.

It might be true to say he had an accountability problem in his organization. It also might be safe to say he's being a bit irresponsible when he doesn't aggressively confront people and problems; in fact, he isn't being *self*-responsible when he lets something go. He knows in his heart there's a little psychological obstacle in his head that blocks him from looking someone square in the eyes, as this chairman did, and asking the person to account for his or her own failure. When this block is active, he's letting himself down.

So if you wanted to improve this situation, what would you do? Most senior leadership teams would demand that the CEO tighten things up. Performance management consultants might come in to see if people know their jobs and if there is alignment from top to bottom in the organization. They would check compensation plans to ensure they were paying people for the right behaviour. Perhaps they'd terminate the CEO.

The board did.

Personally, I would rather have helped the CEO get a grip on his fear of confrontation, particularly since the problematic numbers were going to change direction relatively soon. But it's my job to help people address the obstacles in their heads, so my bias is to find a way to make things work.

In support of the board's decision, one might argue that, for such an important position, focusing on helping the person find greater self-responsibility wouldn't be the swiftest, most responsible thing to do. The board drew the proverbial line in the sand, the CEO stepped over that line, and it was done.

Indeed, terminating the boss is one approach to accountability. And although this book is partly about getting others to fully own or embrace their responsibilities, I strongly believe that a higher authority — a board, an investor, a boss, a team coach, a parent, even a *self* — is smart to sometimes rise above the daily jibber-jabber of who is to blame, what's fair, what's realistic, and just declare, "Nope. This isn't working." Sometimes that's what taking responsibility for the performance of others looks like. It's too bad for the victim, but a profound exercise of free will for the decider.

> A higher authority is smart to sometimes rise above the daily jibber-jabber and just declare, "Nope. This isn't working."

But we're talking about how deciders can dig into an organizational accountability problem rather than just scratch the surface. So let's look at a situation down a few levels in the same organization that just lost the CEO discussed above. In fact, we'll go down eight hierarchical levels to a team leader of a group of accounting personnel — same basic plot, different people.

GETTING TO THE BOTTOM OF IT WITH BRUCE AND LINDA

The supervisor of this team, let's call him Bruce, is also a softie, similar to the CEO who just lost his job. In Bruce's case, a person named Linda has a problem of not doing what she says she'll do. She readily agrees to undertake things, and she's a hard worker who regularly does overtime hours without much recognition and certainly without any extra pay. People respect Linda. But people also complain about her behind her back. Often they'll be in meetings and hear Linda confidently declare something like, "Okay, I'll send that to you this afternoon." And they know Linda just won't do it. It's become, as one person told Bruce, a "pathetic team joke."

Bruce knows about this elephant in the room. He has the same reaction when he hears Linda's promises. A colleague of mine, a coach on my team, asked Bruce about whether he ever discussed the phenomenon with Linda.

"Oh, sure," Bruce said. "Several times. Just last week I probably sent her five or six follow-up emails on things she'd promised — promised in writing! — that never came to fruition."

"And what was her reply?"

"Well, she doesn't always reply, but when she does, it's usually one of five kinds of things: 'Oh, I sent that, but it didn't leave my outbox'; 'I got so caught up in that other crisis we talked about earlier today, I just couldn't get to it'; 'I ran into some problems getting it done because Ernie couldn't find the original documentation'; 'I had to attend to my sick cat/son/mother'; and 'It's on its way.'"

"And have you ever talked about the pattern itself? For example, saying to Linda, 'It sure seems like you often get yourself into that sticky situation where you say you'll do something and then, for any of a bunch of reasons, you ultimately are unable to.'"

"No," he said, but tried to explain. He was afraid Linda would just show how each of the examples was taken out of context and he would end up going around and around with her in an eternal debate. "Without proof," he said, "you can't really hold someone accountable because they wiggle, and if there are realistic, mitigating circumstances, it just doesn't seem fair to play hardball."

"And in the middle, between hardball and eternal wiggling?" my colleague asked.

"There's nothing."

"Is there a price you pay for nothing?"

"Probably some inefficiency. And people do get upset. And I suppose by not acting, people see that people can get away with things. But I have to tell you, Linda really is pretty good at her job overall."

You probably see that there are two great examples of accountability issues being exposed here: Linda's and Bruce's. Should either of them be fired? Probably not. Are systemic initiatives called for? Maybe. An employee survey might uncover mass discontent over people not being held accountable. We could look into whether there's an adequate annual review system whereby employees are given feedback. Compensation plans might be tweaked so that Bruce receives a reward for confronting challenging issues and Linda is given some kind of bonus for stepping up her performance a notch (vis-à-vis fulfilling promises). Increasing the frequency of team meetings might move things toward open communication and thereby greater awareness of mutual support for team members.

But the most productive area of focus would be on the various things going on in their respective heads. Bruce could learn, for example, that there are ways to navigate a dialogue with Linda that would avoid the "wiggle" he's concerned about, and with Bruce's help, Linda could decide whether she's genuinely okay with saying she'll do things and then not doing them — and maybe even decide that she's okay with it, which would then give Bruce the opportunity to decide whether such a decision is all right with him.

WE NEED FEAR AROUND HERE!

There are plenty of people who unfortunately associate accountability with fear of negative consequences, perhaps in the form of losing one's job or even, at a more psychological, often unspoken level, in the form of a physical threat. A common approach to Bruce by such people would be to adopt a militaristic stance, asking Bruce, "What do you mean you haven't confronted Linda about this? For heaven's sake, you're damaging not just your team but the whole organization with this lax stance of yours! And you aren't doing the job of the manager! Management is about control, and you do *not* have things under control!" About Linda, they would warn her that she darn well better do what she says she's going to do or she'll lose her job. It's as simple as that! This isn't a joke!

The problem with this orientation of accountability is that aggression tends to deplete the self-esteem of its victim. And, as we'll see later in this book, there's a direct correlation between healthy self-esteem and a person's sense of willpower — the stuff it takes to do really big things in life, let alone on the job. Another problem with this style of holding people accountable is that it tends to diminish a person's sense of autonomy — when a controlling boss turns up the volume on you doing things the way he or she wants, your feeling of being free to choose can wane and motivation is depleted.

This isn't to say that personal accountability doesn't provoke fear. Indeed, it can feel risky for any of us to shine a light on the inconsistencies in our behaviours and beliefs. But at least it's not a fear of being clobbered — or fired.

> There's a direct correlation between healthy self-esteem and a person's sense of willpower — the stuff it takes to do really big things in life, let alone on the job.

POSING THE BIG QUESTIONS

The essence of accountability lies in requiring people to justify or explain their actions and decisions. As long as that requirement is imposed by a leader in a relatively skillful, essentially non-threatening fashion (supportive, non-judgmental), people navigate toward greater self-responsibility. The types of questions that support the desired culture range from simple check-ins — such as, "Did you manage to … ?" "How did it go?" "How come you took that particular route on this?" — to questions that attempt to unravel the tangles in people's conscious and unconscious thinking that hold them back from being more responsible. We'll consider how to unravel those tangles in Chapters 6 and 7.

> The essence of accountability lies in requiring people to justify or explain their actions and decisions.

For now the point is that questions are the name of the game. They have the power to turn robotic behaviour into moments of clear intention, personal ownership, and uncompromising choice. They can dig at the very heart of full personal responsibility. Put another way, when we say an organization has an accountability problem, or when we hear the cry, "We need more accountability around here!" it's safe to say that people aren't asking or answering, of themselves or of others, what equates to the big, pregnant question: "Why is this behaviour, or this breached commitment, okay?" But a word of caution is in order: beware the paradox of the accountability campaign! The harder you squeeze people for accountability, the less genuinely responsible they become. The key is to tickle responsibility out of people by encouraging self-discovery and inviting people to come clean with themselves.

> The harder you squeeze people for accountability, the less genuinely responsible they become — tickle responsibility out of them by encouraging self-discovery and coming clean with themselves.

BACK TO BRUCE AND LINDA

Bruce was only inches away from admitting to himself that it wasn't really okay to ignore Linda's failed promises. All he wanted was a way to navigate the conversation so that he could avoid the "wiggle." Bruce was indeed asked by my colleague how he could do that. He seized the consultant's suggestion that "It sure seems like you often get yourself into that sticky situation where you say you'll do something and then, for any of a bunch of reasons, you ultimately are unable to." Easy. All it took was some questions, and in this case an idea from a coach.

When Bruce engaged in the conversation with Linda, he was neither pushy nor judgmental. A minute or so after the above statement, he asked, "How come this happens?"

Linda reflected briefly and said, "I guess I'm overloaded."

Bruce replied, "Perhaps. I'd like you to do something about it. What could you do?" She mentioned she could make a note to herself rather than relying on memory. He said, "That could work." And their conversation moved on to other matters.

Bruce knew it would have to be discussed again. Problems such as those he had with Linda don't go away overnight. They are gradually reduced in frequency until new habits are learned and self-awareness is elevated. The next week Bruce asked how the note-taking was going. He checked in with Linda about her feeling of being overloaded. For the next 20 or so weeks, Linda made great progress at revising her personal operating strategy concerning what responsibilities she took on and making notes to herself about her quick promises to others. And her self-awareness concerning the teeny-weeny commitments she made throughout the workday was substantially elevated.

3
COMMITMENT

Here is a brief story about my first exposure to how commitments still work in the real world. Thirty years ago I had my first one-on-one private meeting with an executive vice-president. I had never been exposed to someone with so much authority. We met in his office, which was surely the size of my entire two-bedroom apartment. I was busy taking notes while he spoke about the history of the company and the specific reason for the project. He asked if I had an "org chart." I said I hadn't acquired one yet. He replied, "Okay, I'll get one to you."

That night I was thinking about how a person in such a big and powerful position would get the organization chart to me. Perhaps it would arrive by courier. Maybe his secretary would call and ask how I wished to receive it. Most likely, I thought, it would be placed in an envelope and someone would be sure to give it to me on my next visit to the company's premises.

Not that I'm still waiting, but I never did receive the document. That was my first practical realization that the great and powerful Oz was just a normal guy.

On the other hand, as I type these words, I have someone in mind I would say is very accountable. You can count on her to do what she says, and you can assume that if she slips up, she won't hesitate to declare it. She's not perfect. In fact, when other people allude to how she might be at the root of a particular problem, she doesn't wiggle around to deflect responsibility; instead she simply reflects, explores, admits any role she might have played in the matter, and puts her attention on what needs to happen to prevent a recurrence of the problem. She seems committed to the truth and to doing the job right. People say she's "intense," but while that might be the case, I'd say she's committed.

Of course, people can feel committed to a certain thing at one point in time but not feel the commitment a little later on. But the person I have in mind sustains her sense of commitment over time and seems to have the discipline in her life to fulfill her commitments. Where does this willpower or the ability to sustain a feeling of commitment come from? Notwithstanding the fact that, for various good reasons, some commitments fall by the wayside (times change, for example), why are some people more likely to come through on their word than others? For that matter, what is a commitment? Why do some people resist making commitments? And what's involved in the failure to deliver on a genuinely made promise? Most important, what can we do to improve our own or our team's chances of coming through? These are some of the questions we're about to explore.

For starters, lots of research has been done to determine the factors that influence how likely any of us are to fulfill commitments. It makes sense that psychologists would attempt to put their fingers on humanity's commitment pulse, because to a large extent progress in the world and in an individual depends on people carrying through on their word. Here are the factors that I know of (there are probably plenty more) that influence our fulfillment capacity:

- personal beliefs and values (are they congruent with our commitments?)
- the personal meaning we give to stating our intentions and making promises
- mental health and emotional outlook (for example, willpower can be depleted when we're upset)
- personal history (who taught us how to operate in the world with regards to commitments?)
- alertness (stress and fatigue reduce our capacity)
- innate programming (parents, for instance, may be hard-wired to come through for their kids)
- personal habits (such as writing things down or using reminders)
- current circumstances (the matters that called for a commitment can change)
- availability of support systems (such as corporate performance management systems)
- social pressure (for example, your chances of doing something increase when you announce it)

The first four factors above pertain to our personal mental world and are the ones we're most concerned about in this book — the idea being that people and companies can install all the support tools they want to ratchet up their level of accountability, but without individuals unravelling the tangles in their thinking, they won't be able to go "all the way to clear." Thus, a brief exploration of the psychology of commitment is in order.

> People and companies can install all the support tools they want to ratchet up their level of accountability, but without individuals unravelling the tangles in their thinking, they won't be able to go "all the way to clear."

INTRINSIC VERSUS ADOPTED COMMITMENTS

Making a commitment to ourselves or to others is, or could be, a declaration: I'm going to manage the way the future unfolds. If I don't do this particular thing or fulfill this promise, then things might not go as I intend. In this present moment, I'm *willing* this future. These declarations, if and when they're fulfilled, pretty much define humanity's impact on the world. We get a twinkle in our eyes to accomplish something and we make it happen. We're more certain to make it happen when we make it tangible in some way, such as writing it down or telling someone our intentions. And when we don't carve out some kind of commitment, most of us tend to under-deliver.

> When we intensely feel a commitment we're making, we feel much more resolved. Such commitments seem to come from inside us.

When we intensely feel a commitment we're making, we feel much more resolved. Such commitments seem to come from inside us. Our emotions participate, and sometimes our whole bodies get involved (think of a hand hitting the table: "Well, you can darn well count on *me* to do it!"). Other commitments are made somewhat more loosely.

Consider the line in the diagram that follows as representing degrees of intention or willfulness, with the far right side of the line depicting a very high level of intention or willfulness (for example, protecting your kids), and the far left side of the line depicting a low level (such as vacuuming the floor on a regular basis). Each of the various aspects of your life that might be measured in terms of intensity of intention would fit somewhere on this line. Some of these aspects are listed for your consideration.

We can assume that all commitments we've made or implied in our lives fall into different places on this line, relative to how visceral they feel. Generally, the more instinctual the feeling that accompanies the commitment, the farther to the right it would be on this line and better the chance that the commitment will be fulfilled. Over time, commitments might belong on different places on this line because times, attitudes, and circumstances do indeed change. On the far left, in my case at least, is taking out the garbage on a weekly basis. This happens to be a duty I possess, and I have certainly made the commitment (to my wife) to this mission. Of course, commitments on this side of the line are declarations made or implied that don't possess the same degree of intentionality.

My suggestion is that you determine where each item (following the diagram below) fits on the line so that you can quantify your intentionality toward the items listed and then visualize your intensity about them. Similarly, I also suggest that you consider where other aspects of your life would fit on the line.

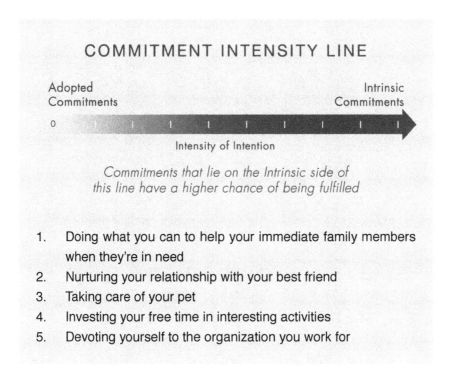

COMMITMENT INTENSITY LINE

Adopted
Commitments

Intrinsic
Commitments

0

Intensity of Intention

*Commitments that lie on the Intrinsic side of
this line have a higher chance of being fulfilled*

1. Doing what you can to help your immediate family members when they're in need
2. Nurturing your relationship with your best friend
3. Taking care of your pet
4. Investing your free time in interesting activities
5. Devoting yourself to the organization you work for

6. Fulfilling your job responsibilities to the best of your ability
7. Taking care of your body
8. Executing a strategy to protect your long-term financial well-being
9. Nurturing your spirituality
10. Protecting the planet
11. Doing the little things you say you'll do

INTRINSIC COMMITMENTS

I'm absolutely committed to the welfare of my family. Nothing will get in the way of that commitment, and I don't at all feel burdened by it. I feel somehow whole because of it — perhaps it's innate. I'm also quite naturally committed to the well-being of my team members. I don't think this commitment is innate, but it does seem to flow naturally, perhaps because I've learned to care about what we do and the people I work with, and possibly because my own livelihood rests on their shoulders. The point is, I don't have to remind myself or muster my internal motivations to feel this commitment. It seems to come from inside me and feels like a driving impulse.

> One key to making a commitment flow naturally, intrinsically, is to connect what must be done to what is genuinely craved.

Something leaders should keep in mind when they seek to motivate employees toward greater commitment is to link or align assignments with what the employee highly values. A cause someone believes in is a good example of what the person values. So, too, would be someone's appetite for a promotion on the job. Aligning assignments in this way tends to increase a person's commitment. For example, if you help me see that trying hard to get a project "just right" will assist me optically in my organization, and I know that how I'm perceived by others is central to my desired next promotion, then I might find myself more committed to getting a project just right. I'll bring more intentionality to the mission. On the other hand, if I don't have that end in mind, my commitment to the project's mission might more easily be distracted. One key to making a commitment flow naturally, intrinsically, is to connect what must be done to what is genuinely craved by the person.

ADOPTED COMMITMENTS

Some of my commitments are positions I've adopted. For example, I'm going to clean up my basement during my next vacation; I promised a colleague I would give her feedback on a regular basis; I'm going to make my company grow by at least 10 percent over the next fiscal year. Regardless of how I became aware of these commitments, the fact is I imposed them on myself. There is nothing wrong with them, and if I gave my word that I would fulfill them, then I'm committed. Adopted commitments are understandably more likely to be breached. For one thing, fulfilling a commitment to something you don't really want to do takes discipline. But even if you're a disciplined person, commitments made lightly don't do so well for any of us. Surely commitments implied but not quite clearly declared tend to have a particularly short lifespan (as in, "Yes, that's what I'm thinking I'll do").

> Adopted commitments are understandably more likely to be breached. Fulfilling a commitment to something you don't really want to do takes discipline.

A LEAP OF FAITH

Logically, all commitments — intrinsic, adopted, and anything in between — require a leap of faith because there are obviously a lot of things going on around us that must work together to make things happen. For example, I can commit to being there at 3:00 p.m., but who knows who is aspiring at this moment to consume my time in the interim.

Another reason a leap of faith is involved is that we can't fully know ourselves. This is big.

"One last kiss and that's it. We have to stop!" I've said those words before. Saying them at the right moment with what seems like profound resolve can, even moments later, due to all sorts of conflicting motives inside us, dissolve like a sugar cube in boiling water. But even when temptation isn't staring us in the face, we still might be smart to avoid dissecting our commitments; doing so can stall momentum. If we give too much attention to possible scenarios in which what we're committing to might not come to fruition, and if we highlight these possibilities in our discussions with others, then we might jeopardize both our own certainty and the confidence of others. So sometimes it's best to be quick about it, ignore the analysis, and just leap.

Picture this effort by a boss to commit to her employee: "You can count on me to be your promoter behind the scenes."

"Really?" the employee perhaps quite logically asks.

"Well, obviously, within reason, of course. I mean, I could leave the company, or senior leadership might turn over, or you could leave the company, or I could get promoted out of this department — all sorts of things could happen. I mean, let's face it. But, basically, yes, you can count on me."

Commitment declarations do require us to block out contingencies. But what's the point of commitment if it's not to overcome obstacles? Most of the time we commit because we know that fulfilling the commitment is going to make things better. Given that such a commitment involves goals worth pursuing, overcoming those obstacles is the responsible or prudent thing to do. Putting ourselves on the hook to get things done is what makes the world move forward.

BAD FAITH

Sometimes leaps of faith are made in bad faith; we aren't consciously fibbing, but we hide some of our truths from our own attention and from other people's. This can happen in a variety of ways. For example, if some part of us knows we have insufficiently considered what work is involved in fulfilling a certain promise, but we run with the part of us that wants to make the promise anyway, then we might succeed socially in the moment but only set ourselves up for future problems. Or if we have conflicting feelings about the subject of a commitment but we commit anyway, there could be trouble.

In fact, bad faith is even brought to bear to avoid committing in the first place. For example, my mother-in-law, regarding the effects of consuming sugar, said, "Don't teach me about it. If you do, I'll have to change." In other words, if I know about this, then I'll feel more responsible than I currently feel and I'll have to commit to more responsible behaviour. Indeed, if we shut our eyes at just the right moment, we can *almost unknowingly* bypass information that would make us responsible.

Why do we have this mechanism in our brains that allows us to hide from our own truths? Nobody knows for sure, of course, but two scientists,

Danny Brower and Ajit Varki, one a geneticist and the other a molecular biologist, describe in their book *Denial: Self-Deception, False Beliefs, and the Origins of the Human Mind* their theory that this capacity evolved as a survival tool. They posit that humanity's advanced brain, with its self-awareness and consciousness of time, grants it absolute certainty that each of us will die. If we didn't have a way to deal with that fact, our despair would get the better of the species as a whole. So we developed neural circuitry that, on a day-to-day basis, enables us to simply look away from the inevitability of our own demise. Presumably we use the same mechanism to deny other thoughts and feelings that don't suit us.

> It's possible that we developed neural circuitry that enables us to look away from the inevitability of our own demise, and that we use the same mechanism to deny other thoughts and feelings.

Regardless of the validity of this theory explaining why we can ignore our truths, in fact, even without knowing about it at all, the philosopher and writer Jean-Paul Sartre wrote a lot about the experience of bad faith, arguing that it comes with being human — built right in, as they say. We're all riddled with conflicting roles, motives, thoughts, and feelings, and inevitably

- our values will conflict with our appetites;
- the demands placed on us can't all be achieved;
- the roles we play at home differ from those we fulfill in our work;
- we hear double messages from employers; and
- we have doubts about whether we actually are what people believe us to be.

The above list of polarities in our consciousness and our tangible lives is certainly personal and probably unlimited. No wonder we have so many adopted commitments versus intrinsic ones. No wonder it's difficult to stay true to our word. No wonder we slide around making commitments. The odds are stacked against people who want greater accountability in their organizations despite their best efforts to align motivations with goals; clarify expectations, objectives, and procedures; and keep people on track.

Fortunately, the process of unravelling the tangles that face us on a daily basis isn't too daunting. Sometimes locating them in our thinking, labelling them, articulating them, and "owning" them can propel us into action. Other times it takes longer, perhaps through a few conversations with oneself or someone else, like a trustworthy friend or boss.

THE PROMISE BREAKERS

So what's *with* the person who almost daily leads people to believe he'll do something, only to develop a consistent pattern over time of just not coming through?

I coached someone who had an employee — we'll call him Bernard — who had this problem. The man I coached wanted help dealing with Bernard and brought me the raw data from Bernard's performance review so that I could see what he was up against. Here is a list of comments that Bernard's colleagues, employees, and customers said about him:

1. All talk, no action.
2. We have to remind Bernard to do the things we agreed on or they just won't get done.
3. I'm so sick and tired of Bernard justifying his broken promises! I've pulled emails with the following excuses: "I pressed Send on my email, but the message got stuck in my outbox," "Our server was down for maintenance," "We ran into technical problems," "I don't remember actually promising that, but I'll be glad to take it on," and "I was led to believe by the mailroom that the package left our office two days ago."
4. If it wasn't for Bernard's creative solutions, we wouldn't be dealing with your organization.
5. How someone can say one minute that he's going to do a certain thing right away, only never to get to it at all is beyond me. This happens so often that I just don't even believe him anymore.

My coaching client had a real problem ahead of him trying to instill a sense of accountability into Bernard. Two years prior, Bernard's previous boss had placed him on probation for this exact problem, but somehow Bernard managed to prove that subsequent breaches weren't his fault and that his creativity and problem-solving skills were too important to lose. So the habits never changed and the probation thing just died out. This was a perfect example of a company that was unsuccessful in creating a culture of accountability.

At Bernard's review, and for a few months thereafter, he and his boss embarked on a series of conversations to get to the root of the problem and try to make things better. The first mission, and it took two conversations to get there, was to get him to acknowledge that, yes, he made a lot of promises he didn't keep, and yes, it looked bad not only on Bernard but also on the department and the company. Most important, Bernard even acknowledged that he wanted to solve the problem because he was embarrassed about it and, despite the fact that he was the culprit, it was against his values.

Before we look at what Bernard's boss uncovered, let's review the basic formula. Bernard became more aware of his motives, problems, and habits and, over time, managed to fix himself. It wasn't from any huge insight, but it did call for increased self-awareness. Bernard became more responsible about only making commitments that he could actually keep (he learned to say no to certain requests), developing personal practices that protected him from falling backward (via a daily prioritized review of his list of promises made), getting help from a couple of colleagues in his department to alert him when he was overcommitting, and becoming more thoughtful when he was saying things that were going to be seen as, or would equate to, a commitment.

The list that follows includes some facts about Bernard he had never looked at squarely, even though he had always been aware of them at some level. When they were brought to light by Bernard, of course, through delicate and persistent questioning from his boss, they had a much less negative impact on his daily behaviour.

1. Bernard likes to please people. He learned as a child that when he promised to do something, his dad seemed to like it. The observation was reinforced for decades — everybody liked him when he said what he'd take on.

2. Bernard was smart enough and fast-thinking enough to stickhandle most complaints about breached commitments that came his way. So the positive reinforcement that he got when he made promises was always greater than the negative reinforcement he faced when someone had him in their sights.

3. Bernard had just slightly more on his plate than he had time to accomplish.

4. Bernard maintained a to-do list only some of the time, but even when he did, he never really organized it based on when things were due. It was just a list of headaches.

5. Bernard was aware that he would look people in the eye and genuinely declare he was immediately going to go do a certain thing, only to walk away and forget about it (seconds later). In fact, all his adult life Bernard thought he had a mild case of attention deficit disorder, which he defined as his attention simply being drawn to the brightest light.

6. Bernard did feel a little "funny" reading about the concerns people expressed in his annual review. He felt some embarrassment about the judgments people made about him, but he "owned" that he was responsible.

7. Bernard admitted that he did tell "little white lies" when he stick-handled people's complaints and that he would feel better if he didn't have to.

The above list is more or less unique to Bernard, but there are probably a billion or so lists similar to it. What it shows, among other things, is that there was no nefariousness, no strangeness, no conscious sabotage, just irresponsibility when it came to keeping his word. The solution for Bernard's boss was to get at these things through non-threatening conversation in a non-judgmental context. Bernard learned to leverage his embarrassment about what people thought about him, and his shame about telling white lies so easily, to motivate himself. Of course, it was too bad that negative feelings had to be used to solve a problem, but in this case they were useful tools, so why not use them? Ongoing conversations with his boss kept the mission front of mind. He developed the habit of writing down every commitment he made, noting its level of importance, reviewing the list daily, and asking his colleagues to keep an eye out for whether he was indeed writing commitments down. Most important, he became progressively better at recognizing the impulse to please, to the point of catching himself mid-sentence and thinking, *There I go again. How remarkable!* His boss now believes the problem has largely been resolved.

THE COMMITMENT ALGORITHM

The level of intensity we bring as we make or hold on to our commitments isn't set by fluke, even though it might seem at any given moment that there is a randomness pertaining to the commitments themselves. There are certain conditions that make it strong, and there are certain factors that detract from intensity.

When I deal with commitment-related issues in my coaching practice, and when my consulting firm guides groups of leaders who are learning about accountability, we present a metaphor that facilitates a rapid understanding of commitment intensity. It involves the positive inputs referred to above powering a beam of light, while the detractors dim that light, such that the net brightness level of the beam reveals the result of the inputs less the detractors. The beam of light might be a metaphor, but what's quite real or tangible is that the various positive inputs and negative influences are indeed electrical circuits in the brain battling it out.

> The level of our commitment is the result of electrical circuits in the brain battling out positive and negative influences.

Positive Inputs

Understandably, a commitment is stronger and we are more likely to chase it when we are attracted to the end state of the fulfilled commitment; for example, when

1. we have strong feelings about how desirable fulfilling the commitment would be (basically, we're able to say, "I really want this");
2. we believe it will simplify our circumstances or even our lives;
3. we see the activity as a source of enjoyment;
4. it is aligned with deeply held values such as a sense of fairness, justice, or goodness;
5. it supports who and what we care about;
6. it will take us closer to what we're trying to accomplish, such as recognition, respect, and positive relations with others; or
7. we think it will help us avoid what we don't want to happen.

In addition to the above inputs, we bring greater intensity to our commitments if we start from a strong sense of self-respect, self-acceptance, and self-esteem (in the non-egocentric sense). We'll consider how this is so in "Willpower," the next chapter. General optimism is also advantageous, both as a starting point as commitment opportunities arise and as we move toward fulfilling the commitments we've already made.

Detractors

But a specific commitment is dimmed if the following detracting feelings and beliefs are at play pertaining to it:

1. Doubts about whether the commitment can successfully be fulfilled
2. The belief that fulfilling the commitment will be meaningless or of low utility
3. Fear that fulfilling the commitment will lead to confrontation (for example, getting into trouble or getting into a fight)
4. Feelings of anger or resentment toward a person whom the commitment involves
5. The perception that the task is boring, uninteresting, or a nuisance;
6. The belief that the activity or task is undesirable due to complexity and the anticipated effort required
7. The opinion that the commitment basically reveals that "change is afoot"

In addition to the above detractors concerning specific commitments, here are backdrop factors that also lessen the intensity of commitments generally:

1. Powerful distractions or a personal vulnerability to distractions;
2. Current high level of anger
3. Preoccupation with other matters
4. Fear of failure or success (and so, perhaps, a general fear of responsibility)
5. Feelings of personal shame
6. A tendency to glibly commit, perhaps as a result of the impulse to please and nurture other people

7. Feelings of insufficient autonomy or that one suffers from a lack of personal control (such that having to commit, in itself, reflects a loss of control)

The whole point here is that, in addition to adopting healthy habits and supports to follow through on promises, we're smart to maximize the positive inputs that inspire intensity — for instance, by articulating how a commitment can be associated with the various energizing inputs — and minimize the intensity detractors. Regarding the detractors, in the previous story about Bernard, great progress was made simply by his articulating the main thematic detractor — his impulse to always please.

*   *   *

But how does one reorient oneself so that commitments are linked to the *positive* inputs that fuel a "brighter" intentionality? Sometimes it's a matter of reminding yourself why you promised yourself or someone else you would do a certain thing in the first place. I might find myself procrastinating about updating a complex spreadsheet because I have lost sight of its purpose. Simply by reminding myself of the pleasure I get when I see a clean data set, I can re-enliven the commitment.

Visualization is another means to orient oneself around the emotional element of an intention. Let's look at an example of my own. For several months more than 30 years ago, I thought about starting my own little consulting business, but I didn't act on it. Then I read a line from Henry David Thoreau's *Walden; or, Life in the Woods*: "If one advances confidently in the direction of his dreams, and endeavors to live the life which he has imagined, he will meet with a success unexpected in common hours." I pulled from these ideas the simple notion of creating an image that I could visualize; in this case, an image of me being a busy consultant. The image was like a snapshot in time: I was in my little apartment walking toward my telephone, with a file folder in my hand, about to pick up the phone. That was the life I imagined, per Thoreau's instruction. I sat in my chair, closed my eyes, and brought this image to mind. I told myself that when I was done I was going to open my eyes and declare to myself: "I am now a consultant." That was the beginning of the "live the life … imagined" part of Thoreau's instruction.

The visualization exercise was 20 minutes in duration and was neither complicated nor particularly profound. I started with the initial image — me moving toward the phone carrying the folder — and populated the image with some subsequent thoughts. I conjured things like what I was wearing, how I was a busy consultant operating out of my home office that day, how I was hearing that telephone ringing, that I was thinking — that the guy in the image was thinking — *Wow! A lot's happening right now.* I brought to mind the pleasure of being a free agent, putting my time where I wanted. And I sat there with the image. Each time I noticed my mind had wandered from the image, I went back to it. I got close to falling asleep, as you might imagine, but managed to keep taking my attention back to the image.

After 20 minutes, I was a consultant. And I did open my eyes and say, "I am now a consultant." I got out of the chair, went to the Yellow Pages book (they had phone books in those days), chose the target market, and called a few places to get started. I set an appointment with a prospective small client within the hour. Twenty-five minutes prior to becoming a consultant, I had no conscious idea of what I would say to prospective clients. At the start of that hour I tried out one pitch, but it didn't work. I changed my descriptions as I went through the calls. It was all very organic.

So what made thinking about being a consultant, and then deciding to be a consultant, into a commitment to be a consultant? Well, indeed, I didn't even use the word *commit*. I didn't say: "I commit to being a consultant." It became a commitment when my "being" changed. The word *being* doesn't have to sound pseudo-spiritual or philosophical in this case; the visualization exercise seemed to merely shift my orientation or my stance, and I made a moment out of it. A 20-minute moment. I had moved from being a wondering wanderer to being a consultant.

Commitments — big commitments, for sure, but little ones, too — are more about *being* than about deciding or declaring. Sure, one decides, and one might indicate or declare, if you will. But the trick to making a commitment is to slow down and mean your words — get the light all the way to bright, so to speak. You must *be* your commitment, or at least allow your sense of self to participate in your commitment. The trick is to take

> Commitments are more about being than about deciding or declaring — the trick is to slow down and mean your words.

the moment. Allow yourself to become your intentionality. Be the chooser as opposed to being the automaton who glibly says what she'll do and who jumps from one thought to the next.

You don't need to invest a long moment when you give your word. It's a matter of learning to detect, when you're uttering some kind of intention to act, that you are, indeed, giving your word and that, therefore, you have to mean it. Perhaps it would be a tenth of a second? It doesn't have to take 20 minutes to become the person who promises to call Billie back tomorrow. Try to find some emotion or feeling around the topic you're committing to. Emotion is the source of motivation. For example, if you know you should buy flowers for your partner but you keep procrastinating, locate inside yourself the why behind your intention. Perhaps it is to demonstrate love. Or it is the desire to make him or her feel loved. Focus on the feelings, and they will help you to shift the commitment you've made to yourself along the commitment line from the adopted end closer toward the intrinsic end.

I would argue that *emotion is the secret sauce of making a commitment.* Emotions tap into a person's being. It's not a coincidence that the root of the words *emotion, motivation,* and *motion* is the Latin root *movere* ("to move"). Emotions are the source of motivation insofar as we tend to do things we think will lead to a positive feeling such as satisfaction or happiness. The various positive inputs in the commitment algorithm each pertain to feelings or emotions.

This also points to the biggest reason people procrastinate: they don't feel much *oomph* about the task they're "sitting on." Procrastinators (all of us, really, since we all procrastinate about *some* things) are well advised to orient themselves around the positive feelings that will ensue from completing a task that has undesirable elements to it.

WHAT YOU CAN DO TO IMPROVE YOUR COMMITMENT SKILLS

Now let's look at some practical tools to help anyone who has a problem making or fulfilling commitments. Many of the steps prescribed below link to the tangles that might underlie the problem. We're going to address various common tangles later in this book, but what follows is a good place to get started.

Trouble Committing

Locate the parts of you that are at battle. For example, I spoke recently to someone who found himself putting off a marriage proposal. The secret he couldn't tell his girlfriend was that there was a part of him that wanted to keep himself available in case he found someone better. He was conflicted between his love and respect for his current partner, plus his knowledge that formalizing their union was pretty much inevitable, and the fact that he was secretly keeping his eye on the romance marketplace. By discussing his belief that there might be someone better, and the origin in his life of such a thought pattern, he realized he didn't have to be driven by it.

Another example features a 30-year-old working in the advertising world who hated his job. But he couldn't start looking for another position and found himself unable to talk to his boss about why he didn't like his job. He went home every day filled with anger — at the people around him and at himself for being such a "wimp" about it (afraid of confrontation with his boss). He couldn't get himself to act on the problem. However, by taking the pressure off the need to commit to action and instead just exploring the various things he could actually do about the problem if he wasn't so fearful of acting, he got to the bottom of his inaction and came up with the exact non-adversarial way he needed to communicate his concern to his boss. As soon as his boss found out how the fellow felt, the problem was solved.

To get past the reluctance to commit, we need to get to the bottom of it. We should ask ourselves the following:

- Is it about not being able to predict the future? Predictability is very desirable for all of us. But when you hop in your car, you face unpredictability there, too. Remind yourself that, just as you know you'll deal with whatever comes up on the road ahead, you'll also be able to deal with the consequences of moving into this commitment. Meanwhile, as a way to move forward, consider accepting the fear as an appropriate response to the situation and as an invitation to take small steps to mitigate that fear.
- Is it about losing control? Indeed, diving into something can feel as if you're forfeiting freedom. Explore how you can use the commitment to your advantage in some way. Ask yourself what, in the mid- and long term, is better for you and for those you love.

- Is it a fear of failure? Fear of success? Articulating your fears, considering what you would do if things didn't go well, embracing fears, and developing a list of baby steps might get you through it. The old psychotherapeutic adage regarding strong feelings such as fear is "name it, frame it, tame it." That is, by accepting that you have the fear and getting to know exactly what it is you're afraid of, you'll tame it. Awareness, or bringing the fear into the light, will go a long way.

- Is it deep-down, private laziness? Taking on a commitment is, perhaps by definition, work. Focus on the feelings you'll have (pride, benefit for others, income, improvements around you) when you finally fulfill the commitment — and get to it.

Whatever you discover through this thinking process, what small action can you take that will bring you a little bit closer to your goal? Perform that action, but nothing too big. After you've done so — taken that baby step — do it again. Inch yourself toward the thing you don't want to commit to or the commitment you don't want to fulfill. Can you find a way to link what you really want in the near-, mid-, or long term to the thing you're reluctant to commit to? The more carefully you align your commitments with what you seek deep down, the more responsibly you'll handle yourself.

Committing but Not Fulfilling

Some people will promise to do anything merely to keep things rolling in a conversation. If you're one of those people, it would be smart to consider the consequences — to other people, to yourself, and to your organization. Keep track of your promises. Have a place where you record them, and develop the habit of looking at the list regularly. If you have some kind of software you can use to alert you to due dates, use it. But be sure you don't get into the habit of ignoring the alerts that pop up on your screen.

Try only to make promises you know you can keep. If you have a big problem with making too many promises, get into the habit of saying no. Look back at recent failed commitments to detect a pattern: are there certain types of things you indicate you'll do but don't? Those are the commitments to stop making, to make more thoughtfully, or for which you should unpack what tangles are underneath. For example, ask yourself: Why am I consistently getting into this mess? Is it because I'm overloaded? Trying to please? Self-sabotaging? Feeling pressure to comply? Genuinely unable to do what must be done? Attempt to locate a theme in your answers that you can address. Ask for help from colleagues when they catch you agreeing to do things that are unrealistic. Even if you can't accomplish what you've promised, be sure to let people know in advance of when they expect completion that there will be a delay. This will help you to manage the optics of overpromising and under-delivering.

Sit down and confront the fact that each time you breach a promise, you're committing a moral offence against others and doing yourself a disservice. Own the deception. Sure, you will and should forgive yourself for your past indiscretions (we're sure your heart is in the right place), but let the essential culpability sink in. When you forgive yourself, feel compassion for the part of you that's been breaching promises. Let the part of you that feels that compassion be the part of you that comes to your rescue the next time you're about to promise something unrealistically. Let the compassion inform your choice to reduce the load you're taking on.

If you're a person who has a wide list of things to do that are seemingly of equal importance (I call that a "horizontal value system"), try to sort the list vertically, with the most important things to do at the top. Often a person will allow a horizontal value system to take over because he or she isn't using intuition to "value" each item in relation to its importance in the grand scheme of things. Re-sorting the list can make someone far more productive, on the principle that doing important things first will lead to fewer unimportant matters arising. Finally, consider finding ways to lock yourself into fulfilling a commitment. For example, tell people your commitments, because doing so will make you feel more accountable.

WHAT YOUR ORGANIZATION CAN DO TO ENHANCE COMMITMENT

So, with our eyes back on the question of how organizations can develop a culture of accountability, beyond systemic tools such as ensuring people know what they have to do and closely monitoring performance, they also need to create a context for responsible performance on the job vis-à-vis commitment. It's generally important to make sure people buy into the values, mission, and vision of their organization. If team members can see and feel the "why" of what they do, they'll approach their roles with a sense of being responsible for doing it well. The following actions can also enhance commitment:

- Engage people in setting their own targets. Imposed targets tend to deplete the sense of autonomy, while embraced, self-established targets become intrinsic commitments.
- Talk with people about why they're committing. Ensure they actually believe in their alleged resolutions.
- Use conversation to anticipate the obstacles the person might face in the fulfillment of the commitment and what the person will do about those obstacles.
- Help people to realize they're valued and able. That is, give them genuine positive feedback and encouragement. This will enliven their sense of self-worth and ability and make them more willful.
- Avoid the use of fear to drive a commitment.
- Engage people emotionally in their commitments, knowing that motivation is derived from emotion. This is the essence of genuine inspirational leadership.
- Devise systems that gently remind people of their commitments. For example, ask them during one-on-one conversations with you how they're progressing against their commitments.
- Align, as much as possible, compensation, job descriptions, and task assignments with the employee's personal beliefs and commitments.
- Participate in employee commitments as much as you can by making your own commitments to help.
- Ensure that the systems and people that associate with your team member actually support or are at least congruent with the commitments your team member has made.
- Make a "thing" about commitment in your organization, such that it's part of your culture and what you value.
- Resist conversations in your organization about who is to blame. Instead, stay focused on what can be done in the future. In fact, applaud mistakes, because people learn by making mistakes.

> If team members can see and feel the "why" of what they do, they'll approach their roles with a sense of being responsible for doing it well.

- Talk about your own commitment. Invite people to highlight when you or your colleagues are behaving inconsistently with commitments that have been made. Seek to explore, rather than defend.
- Compensate for the natural tendency of commitment to wane ("commitment entropy") by revisiting (providing reminders of) group and individual commitments, applauding successes, and seeking to learn from failures.
- Solicit realistic commitments, rather than stretch promises that aren't likely to be fulfilled.
- Participate in group and individual victories so that the core feelings of self-responsibility are reinforced. Commitment is sustained through genuine positivity.
- Remember that commitment comes from one's sense of self or one's being and that creating positive energy around that sense tends to elevate commitment — celebrate successes, celebrate the individual, resist judgment, have fun, and play together.

Now, before we explore willpower in the next chapter, let's collect our thoughts about what we've covered in this chapter.

SUMMING UP

The capacity to commit implies the possibility of self-deception. For small matters and big ones too, we give our word so that we can fulfill a vision of how we want the world to unfold, but in giving our word, we make a leap of faith insofar as we don't actually know how things will unfold. This capacity to leap, as critical as it is for willing the future, also happens to enable us to make unreasonable and unrealistic leaps and to hide certain truths from ourselves that can ultimately block us from doing what we genuinely intended in the first place.

> We mitigate the risk of self-deception by bringing more of ourselves to our commitments.

We mitigate the risk of self-deception by bringing more of ourselves to our commitments. We could say that attempting to shift commitments closer to the intrinsic end of the "Commitment Intensity Line" makes them "come from the heart." This can be done in several ways. We can

- visualize the fulfillment of a goal or promise to amp up our ambitions;
- associate feelings and emotions with our commitments;
- look at any thoughts at the periphery of our awareness that might be relevant to our commitments in order to uncover polarities or other cognitive stances that might unwittingly hold us back; or
- employ basic tools that bring our attention back to the goal.

Making and keeping commitments is critical for any organization that wants to elevate its sense of cultural accountability, not just because people use commitments to shape the future rather than let things unfold organically, but also because commitments are the preconditions of genuine accountability. Accountability requires all people managers to nurture the unfolding of personal responsibility in each individual in the community. This unfolding comes not from the imposition of accountabilities, but from cultivating the alignment of individual personal goals with organizational mandates, and from celebrating the *being* of each employee.

4
WILLPOWER

What would you do differently if you had more willpower? I informally asked 10 people in a row, and here are their responses:

1. I would exercise more.
2. I would confront the people who bug me rather than hide from confrontation.
3. I would cook dinner more often.
4. I would do my reports the day before they are due instead of rushing around on the due date.
5. I would book reviews with my employees rather than procrastinate.
6. I would improve my work–life balance.
7. I would get more education. There is a course I've been thinking of taking.
8. I would reduce my alcohol consumption.
9. I tend to be late for everything. I would get a grip on that problem.
10. I would quit my job and freelance.

After hearing each answer, I asked, "And what would you do if you were a more personally responsible person?" Although their answers might have been biased by the recency of the previous question, each said, "Same thing."

Indeed, I believe we all know that being personally responsible means having the willpower to do what some bigger part of us believes or has been conditioned to believe we ought to do. Think about it: all of the people above know that what they really want lies just underneath their appetites and day-to-day distractions. They have a sense of what's right, or what's good for them, or how they would like their world to unfold, but they haven't quite mastered their distractions. At least up to the moment of the question, they have lacked the willpower.

Willpower is the ability to resist short-term temptations in order to meet long-term goals. But where does that ability come from?

At the surface, willpower shows up as having strategies to deal with the various temptations life has to offer. At its core, I am pretty sure willpower "flows" from, or is closely associated with, a sense of self. I know that people with high self-esteem, for example, tend to do better on tests of willpower (one such test measures how long one can hold a hand in freezing water).

Somewhere between the surface-level tricks of the trade and the well-spring itself are the tangles that block its greater flow. We'll explore how that works in Chapter 6. In this chapter, we'll look into various temptation management strategies specifically and the impact of self-esteem on willpower. But first an example to get the big picture.

I woke up this morning knowing I "should" exercise, but darn if I wasn't up late last night and didn't sleep well. The situation this morning called for willpower to overcome my desire to skip exercising today. Now, I am reasonably in touch with my desire to exercise, and it's pretty significant. I basically fear that if I'm not in shape, then I'll die sooner. So, although I felt the temptation to just not do it, after only a few seconds of indecision, perhaps aided by the fact that I've trumped this exact temptation thousands of times, I was up and making my way to the elliptical machine — even though there was still a part of me that didn't want to.

Prior to getting my head straight about daily exercise, I would have a battle in my head, and, against my better judgment, I would usually give in to the easy option. I experienced years of this personal challenge, of failed efforts to suppress my desire to be lazy. What follows is a brief, real life examination of the three layers referred to above: surface strategies at the top, self-esteem issues at the bottom, and the thought tangles in the middle.

First, I learned to take advantage of what I already knew about how I personally tend to deal with temptation. For instance, I told people I was committed — basically, so I would feel embarrassed if I failed. I made getting to the exercise facility as easy as possible by putting it in my basement. I started going to bed earlier so I would have more idle time in the morning, betting on the hunch that if I were bored, I would be much more likely to just do it. And I tracked what I did and how long I did it to heighten my awareness and create a context for competing against myself — for example, do better than yesterday. I love to measure and benchmark my performance.

Second, regarding self-esteem, I tried to accept who I am and ultimately bring more clarity to my experience of self. We'll soon see that willpower is strengthened when traits such as self-efficacy and self-acceptance are heightened. A handy thing to know when you're leading people is that when you make them feel smaller after you've spoken to them, because, for example, of a subtle judgmental style you sometimes reveal, they have measurably less willpower but might have more anger. However, when you help them perceive themselves as able and, through your acceptance of their humanity, worthy — the two beliefs that are necessary to self-esteem — they have more willpower.

Third, by untangling some conflicting thoughts, I put my finger on the real reason I should exercise: people in my family die at relatively young ages, and I know that exercise doesn't guarantee anything, but it does tend to prolong life. The wrestling match in my head, the tangled-up thoughts that blocked me from action, equated to a simple polarity: life or laziness. I had always been a fan of slothful ways, but I knew it came from a much shorter-term point of view. Untangling these thoughts meant realizing I had been procrastinating not just because exercising was work, but also to hide from the point that basically my life was at stake. I had been in bad faith. Shining a light on it dissolved it.

Done. For over 15 years I've exercised pretty much six times per week — 5.6, to be exact, because, as we'll see, for some people keeping track can bring a goal into focus.

So, as promised, let's look at two of the three ingredients in more detail in this chapter. First, we'll delve into the surface-level elements of habits, behaviours, tools, and tricks. Then we'll dive into the deepest level, the source of willpower, and in Chapter 6, we'll explore the third ingredient: how to unblock the obstacles that, by virtue of the conflicting beliefs they represent, tend to lock us up.

HABITS, BEHAVIOURS, TOOLS, AND TRICKS

The theory of emotional intelligence, still fairly young in the history of psychology, highlights that emotionally savvy people do, indeed, face temptation but somehow manage to work around it, pre-empt it, or visualize it differently.

They have learned the tricks of the trade, if you will. In other words, if you love marshmallows but are trying to resist them and one is sitting in front of you, it's been proven that you should simply look away rather than stare the confection down. Researchers have shown this over the past 20 years in multiple ways.

We're going to consider only a few of these techniques. Several of them fall into the category of commitment devices, and we'll review that concept and a few examples. Then we'll glide through a short list of others, some of which won't be new to you, which is why we'll be brief. After that we'll get to the bottom of willpower by examining its relationship with self-esteem.

Commitment Devices

People use commitment devices to incentivize or lock themselves into doing the thing they promise. These methods can help, but they aren't guaranteed. For example, you might be committed to discontinue reviewing social media while you're at work, so you remove the corresponding bookmarks to make it easier to resist. That could, indeed, work for a while, but with the push of one button in a moment of weakness, things could return to normal.

My first personal experience with a commitment device was as a little boy who didn't get enough sleep. It was a serious problem by the time I got to grade seven. I would wake up in the morning to my alarm clock, simply bang it off, and go back to sleep. After a year or so of this, I learned the trick of hiding my alarm clock on the other side of the room under a chest of drawers. That way, to stop the alarm, I had to get out of bed, crawl across the room, and reach under the chest for the clock to put an end to the noise. The remote positioning of the clock was the commitment device. It worked quite well until I couldn't take it anymore and started sleeping in again.

Actually, I believe I thought of this device because I had learned that even the legendary Greek king of Ithaca, Odysseus, tied himself to the front of his ship to avoid the temptation of the sirens, though I didn't really know what that was about at the time. But the point is that using commitment devices isn't new to humanity; Homer was on to it more than 2,000 years ago.

A very simple but effective commitment device is to simply tell yourself exactly what you will say or do when temptation strikes so you can sidestep a recurring problem. For instance, knowing that you easily fall prey to invitations to have dessert after a meal, you might plan a future response that will protect you from initially giving in. You might say, "No, thanks. I can't eat dessert." Or as we'll see later in this chapter, it might be better to say, "I don't eat dessert." The point is that the planned response pre-empts the impulse to just say yes.

Even contracts are a form of commitment device. When people sign their names to a commitment, they're more likely to fulfill it. The belief is that as time passes, circumstances change, and conflicting impulses emerge, the commitment device is in place to keep things on course. Corporate policies can also be used to guard against impulsive decisions. Companies make rules, for example, about the limits service personnel must stay within when customers seek special favours.

A senior leader I coached had a problem with confrontation. One manager on his team had some bad habits (such as always coming to the team's defence rather than providing directional leadership); his boss tended to be critical of him at senior meetings, and my client didn't really know why; and other departments weren't fulfilling their promises. It was evident to him that his fear of confrontation was affecting his performance. His commitment device was simple, and it worked. Each time he had a one-on-one meeting booked with an individual with whom he had to address various issues, he made it a personal policy to type into the subject field of his calendar entry a polite one- or two-word reference to the matter he wanted to raise. Because his calendar entries were accessible by not just him but also the person he was meeting with, he was locking himself into the sensitive conversation.

How do commitment devices help to create a culture of accountability? Enabling people to fulfill their commitments to themselves and to their organization builds momentum around not just corporate accountability but also personal responsibility. Accomplishing goals creates positive momentum toward even greater willpower and, surely, tangible results.

Tricks of the Trade

Here is a brief description of other means by which emotionally intelligent people exercise their willpower skills:

1. **Avoid temptation.** Pretty much the exact opposite of commitment devices are efforts to avoid temptation in the first place.[1] For instance, if you eat candies at the office and want to stop, don't sit there battling with them — remove them.

2. **Divide longer tasks into baby steps.** When busy people take on strategic initiatives, it's difficult to weave those initiatives into their schedules, so it's easy to fall off track. By dividing a mission into a series of subtasks, one is less likely to procrastinate.

3. **Count and measure.** There is all sorts of evidence that measuring performance tends to highlight what's required to go all the way to fulfilling objectives. When people know how they're doing versus goals, they can self-adjust, compete against previous performance, and compete with others. Targets properly laid out can inspire us to keep our eye on the ball.

4. **Create frequent reminders.** Don't underestimate the research that shows willpower can be sustained longer when one has frequent reminders of the goal.[2]

5. **Interpret failures optimally.**[3] Skillful willpower users see individual failures as localized (rather than necessarily invading every aspect of their lives), not necessarily recurring, and not actually totally attributable to them alone. Slip-ups are inevitable and surely are only one part of the big scheme of things behind making serious change. They need to be seen in perspective.

6. **Use self-talk to self-regulate.** Go ahead, yell at yourself, out loud when necessary, if you're sitting in front of sumptuous food you know you have to stop eating: the part of you who wants to eat, whose circuitry lives in some corner of your brain, might just comply. Similarly, when you're feeling guilty for your willpower slip-ups, tell yourself you forgive the indiscretion you've committed. Indeed, it's safe to assume the wiser part of you literally lives in a different place in your head than the area that speaks for temptation.[4] One can program the other. For example, by learning to say, "I don't eat sweets," instead of, "I can't eat sweets," you can trick your brain into thinking that eating sweets simply doesn't fit who you are, rather than how eating sweets is something that has to be clamped down on.[5]

7. **Imitate the confidence of others.** If you know powerful people, you can pretend you feel just as powerful and thereby increase your chances of overriding your "lesser" impulses.

8. **Avoid "willpower depletion."** Psychologists have studied this phenomenon whereby willpower temporarily dwindles due to overuse.

So, promising yourself massive personal change is usually pretty ineffective because you might not have the *oomph* to execute. By the way, we can compensate for willpower depletion by increasing and balancing our glucose levels (but avoiding refined sugar), elevating mood, and reconnecting with the motivation for the commitment we're working to fulfill.

EXPERIENCING WILLPOWER

Think about it: do you ever find using willpower to be an on-the-spot pleasurable experience? I doubt it. Afterward, maybe, but at the moment of willpower overruling a behaviour, it's not really much fun. Actually, if willpower were something that gave us instant gratification, it probably wouldn't be a human challenge in the first place — we'd be positively conditioned to check our impulses simply because it felt good!

Personally, when I have an appetite for something but ultimately override the appetite, there is an "aw, shucks" element in the moment. It's as though I were back in grade school, inclined to do one thing but being told to "settle down" by a higher authority. And if I ever do just overrule an appetite with only a little regret, it's usually because I feel sufficiently "programmed" to do so. I personally doubt there's any heroism involved in those circumstances.

No doubt about it: willpower is work.

Our mission together is to address self-esteem as the source of willpower and to turn up our better judgment's level of influence over our appetites. We've already spoken of the various tools at our disposal, such as commitment devices, and techniques, such as saying the right things to ourselves, but how do we get underneath?

I AM NOT MY APPETITES

The first thing we have to do in our analysis is put temptation in its place. Now that science allows us to peer inside the brain while people think and experience things, it is known that the part of us that houses our better judgment — the prefrontal cortex — is physically separate from the brain's limbic system, where our more animal appetites are found. So, for example, if you find yourself terribly bored during a meeting, feel the impulse to put your attention elsewhere, or have an urge to walk out, your impatience likely corresponds with the section of the brain that wants what it wants, while your "thinking brain" knows better.

There is a great utility in learning to recognize such appetites while they're happening. It would allow you to gain perspective, to see them in the light of the bigger picture. But without gaining that outlook, we tend to fall prey to the allure of those appetites. Psychologists (for example, Roberto Assagioli[6] and Piero Ferrucci[7]) call that "identification," the experience of identifying oneself with a certain point of view. That is, almost or somehow "becoming" the experience, in the same sense that we say, "I am overly identified with my job." The latter means that the job has "consumed me" and I have lost my perspective on life. They point out that we lose some strength when we're identified with a relatively narrow point of view. Along the same lines, our strength increases when we regain our broader perspective, which is where willpower resides. Creating a psychical distance from distractions and temptations promotes greater control.[8] Put differently, the prefrontal cortex of the brain has been seen as the home of our sense of time and morality and is the area of the brain that reflects on life and long-term goals; when it's in control of our attention, we're more centred, less likely to let our appetites run free.[9]

> Learning to recognize appetites while they're happening allows you to gain perspective, to see them in the light of the bigger picture, and to avoid falling prey to their allure.

Even our language sets us up to identify ourselves as something. I am a gardener. I am a lawyer. I am a trainer. I am "just" *xyz*. I am hungry. We even identify with our hunger! (But in French one says I "have" hunger, so at least when it comes to food, francophones have one less thing they need to burden themselves with.) But in truth we're never just one thing. We're many things, hopefully all integrated. There is an illusion at play when we identify with one thing alone. You aren't your job; you merely have a job. You aren't your toothache; you have a toothache. You aren't your emotions; you have emotions.[10] You aren't your stress; you have stressors. You aren't your shame; you merely have shame.

You are your will. You are the chooser. You aren't the weakling who wants chocolate cake; you are the agent who's going to make a choice.

How do we shift our attention to that bigger perspective?

1. **Label our experiences while we are having them.** For instance, back in that meeting, "This is me being impatient." Or "This is my avoidance tendency in action." There are at least as many such labels in the world as there are humans on the planet. But the act of naming tends to loosen us up from the shackles of our attention.

2. **Find your quiet place.** If you make a regular practice of taking five to ten minutes, even just once a day, to simply slow down your thoughts so that you feel you have more "space" in your awareness rather than fast-dancing clutter, that mental space will strengthen your capacity for "detached observation."[11]

3. **Look at yourself.** If you stand and gaze back at where you were sitting, as prescribed by some Gestalt therapists, and pretend you're still seated there, you can physically induce disidentification. And you can describe what that person sitting there (you) is going through. You can even give advice; doing so equates to the bigger-perspective-you speaking with the narrower-perspective-you — you're suddenly free of the identification and are able to gain some perspective.

4. **Write to yourself.** Keeping a diary record of what you're experiencing at a particular time of "overidentification" (when it's especially difficult to defixate) can help you gain perspective. Just let your thoughts go, writing or typing as fast as you can. The act of putting experiences to words, perhaps just because of the subject/object syntax of grammar, tends to produce the space required for a better vantage point.

5. **Distract yourself.** We all know that if we sleep on it, we'll likely wake up with a slightly bigger and more relieved view of things. Music, physical activity, and immersion in activity can all have the same effect.

I AM ABLE AND WORTHY

Okay, so you aren't your temptation. You can be accessed via your prefrontal cortex. (Don't ask me where your sense of *you* is, because I just don't know.) You periodically have the gift of perspective. Here's the next main point: your ability to regain perspective is influenced by how you feel about yourself. When self-esteem is stronger, there is a greater sense of will despite the allure of contrary impulses. And when it's not as powerful, there is diminished ability to self-manage or use willpower. So the target person — you or the person you want to support — benefits profoundly from increased self-esteem.

We're using the term *self-esteem* in a somewhat informal sense in this book. We're simply referring to people feeling fairly good about themselves. Self-esteem was defined early on as the experience of two beliefs. The belief that "I am able" suggests self-efficacy — that I am confident I can deal with what life delivers. The "I am worthy" belief points to being deserving of respect and being valued by others and oneself.[12] It's a powerful pair of notions to honestly report to oneself.

The concept of self-esteem did get its share of resistance not too long ago when, for example, parents and educators focused so hard on boosting self-esteem that people began to score high on narcissism. "I am worthy" and "I am able" morphed into "I am entitled." But the spirit or essential meaning didn't wane: when you feel good about yourself, you tend to have more willpower. If you feel a lot of shame (as in, "I am at the core not a good person"), then you'll have lower agency or less willpower or, for our purposes, less self-esteem. But if you accept yourself, stay relatively humble, feel valued by others, and are empowered to make decisions, then you'll have *more* willpower.

> When self-esteem is stronger, there is a greater sense of will despite the allure of contrary impulses.

All of us — ourselves, our kids, our employees — need to feel we're unfolding, not shrinking. We must feel connected to what we want for ourselves, not blocked from it or distracted by it. We must operate in an environment where we can trust the people around us to be rational, fair, relatively predictable, friendly, and freeing (so that we may feel our autonomy). If our environment suffers in any of these ways, we'll experience less willpower.

This is one of the problems for some organizations that seek a greater sense of accountability. They often install systems to track performance and miscommunicate the intention, causing people to feel less freedom to act. They decide they must confront people for failed performance — that is what accountability is all about, right? — and do it in such a way that a culture of fear emerges. They install "key performance indicators" without consulting the people who have to achieve them, and they generate resentment. Resentment doth not empowerment make.

My experience is that the desire for a culture of accountability, whether it's the desire of management or of a peer group, unfortunately goes hand in hand with the inclination to judge. When people feel judged for who they are rather than what occurred, their self-esteem shrinks, their willpower declines, their tendency to take healthy risks plummets, they build up resentment, and the accountability mission fails. Indeed, it is the job of managers to judge, but the skill of leadership is to assess performance without sending signals of having judged the person.[13] In fact, it takes willpower on the part of a leader to resist the natural temptation to judge the person rather than the behaviour. So a good leader needs willpower to support the willpower of team members. Indeed, there is a virtuous circle embedded in this. Rather than driving toward imposed accountability, we're more graceful when we adopt a results orientation that also integrates: respecting the humanity of the people around us; resisting the temptation to judge people instead of behaviour; creating a culture of consistent, fair, ethical behaviour; fashioning a convivial work environment; and nurturing personal responsibility for each person in our circle. More achievement leads to more self-esteem, and more self-esteem achieves better results for everyone.

DO THINGS YOU DON'T WANT TO DO

We said before that willpower is like a muscle; it can tire out from overuse. But the good news is that the reverse is also true. You can actually elevate your own self-esteem simply by doing things you don't want to do. We're talking about more baby steps here, not just in parsing a task into smaller components but in exercising the muscle of willpower. Megan Oaten and Ken Cheng discovered when they asked people to perform small acts of willpower, such as refusing a piece of cake or doing some physical exercise, that their subjects increased their ability to concentrate and solve a hard problem despite distractions.[14]

In the book *The Road Less Traveled and Beyond* by M. Scott Peck, the author makes what I still think to be an amusing but insightful point. He suggests that he was sad to discover at some point in the course of his life that the key to mental health is, basically, denying yourself pleasures. Peck explains that he was a man of pleasure, and the basic rule is that pleasure has to be limited.[15] Indeed, how deflating! But I must say that after experimenting with essential hedonism in previous decades of my life, I have landed in essentially the same spot. The practice of overcoming impulses seems to be a gateway drug not just to discipline but also to a sense of being the chooser rather than the robot. That is perhaps our quest here: becoming choosers and helping the people who wish to be supported to become choosers, as well.

> You can actually elevate your own self-esteem simply by doing things you don't want to do.

Okay, so let's put the elements of these views of willpower and a couple of nuggets from the previous chapter on commitment together:

1. At the surface level, there are some tricks of the willpower trade: things like commitment devices, avoiding temptation outright, planning baby steps, measurement, frequent reminders, managing our interpretations of our slip-ups, and using our self-talk to self-regulate.

2. We do get stuck on or identify with our distractions — the things that block us from doing what we want to do.

3. We're less likely to get stuck if a given commitment we've made connects intrinsically (for instance, we have strong feelings about it), because the commitment will be informed not just by our executive-thinking centre in our brain, but by our limbic system, as well. It will be a stronger commitment and more likely to be fulfilled.

4. The frequency at which we link, or our leader links, what needs to be done with what we *want* to do (limbic system) will affect how likely we are to stay on track.

5. If we can gain perspective when we're hooked by distractions and actually see ourselves with some measure of objectivity, perhaps by

naming our experience, we'll likely shift out of identification with the distraction and be released.

6. We can regain that perspective on the spot with certain exercises, such as labelling what we've identified with.

7. We can generally improve our ability to go back and forth between the subject of our attention (the thing we've identified with) and our larger perspective by elevating our self-esteem. We tend to approach things with greater perspective when we feel good about ourselves.

8. Our leaders can help by being non-judgmental and by genuinely supporting the view that we're worthy and able. They can make us feel "bigger" rather than "smaller."

9. We can help ourselves by practising doing things we don't want to do. This exercises the muscle. It helps us be the chooser rather than the robot.

5
FREE OF BLAME

This is a very personal story, which I would like to share to set the stage for our discussion of blame. It's about the uselessness of blame.

My mother's body was laid out in the basement of the funeral home, and I was allowed a few minutes alone with her. The funeral director stayed in the doorway, half in the room to supervise me, I guess, and half out of the room to grant me some privacy.

I'd had a lot of problems in my relationship with my mother, and I spent most of my first three decades blaming her for my innumerable insecurities, just as I believe she had blamed me for invading her life in the first place. My experience of our relationship suffered many difficult phases, ranging from despair over thinking I wasn't loved, to shame for being an allegedly bad person, to anger at her for what I labelled her self-ishness, to guilt for treating her badly, to regret for what could have been, and, ultimately, to release. The release part occurred a few years prior to her death, after which we had only had perfunctory conversations more or less dictated by social circumstance.

This time alone with her on the day of her death was somewhat one-sided. There she was lying motionless, eyes closed, having just departed, and I was in a position to say whatever I wanted. Was it to be motivated by anger? Pain? Guilt? Sadness would surely have been appropriate. Actually, the best word I can use to describe my emotional state at the time is *clean*. Probably the cleanest I've ever felt. I had arranged this private visitation to see what would come up from the depths of my unconscious. Perhaps, I thought, and contrary to what I had come to believe, I hadn't, in fact, pro-cessed all of the significant emotion-based complexities of my relationship with my mother. So I stood there, waiting. It seemed to be just 30 seconds. My eyebrows went up and I said to her, "Well, there you go."

It might sound like there was an edge of "I won" or "I told you so" in the statement, but I don't think I was coming from a place of opposition. It was more like, "This is how it all ended up. After all that, after all the blame, the wrestling for responsibility, the helplessness, the defence, things basically turned out as one would expect."

I turned to the man and walked out of the little room. I heard the door close behind me as I ascended the stairs.

I don't blame my mother anymore. Not at all. I realize she was what she was, and, in truth, among other things, she was brave and loving. Probably once a year even still I have a loving memory of different childhood moments of joy in her presence. I also realize there's no need for blame. My blame got "spent," or exhausted. I was clear. And done. Nothing left but the facts and to pick up the pieces. Take full responsibility for myself, my body, my feelings, my actions.

I wouldn't wish this cold end to a mother–child relationship on anyone, but I'm grateful for having found peace through the whole arduous process. Today I would probably have been in better touch with my compassion during, and at, her life's end, but that's a fairly recent lesson. A lesson I learned some time ago, and which I still hold onto firmly, is that blame might be a natural response, but it's surely a waste of time. And time wasted is life-time wasted, if you know what I mean.

Needless to say, blame, at least in the sense that it's usually loaded with emotional judgment or defence, is also hurtful. And I can see no good reason, all things considered, for causing hurt to others.

WIRED FOR BLAME

It's one thing to sort out the various contributing factors in a problem — in fact, it's natural — but it's another thing to let that motivation devolve into blame. My stance in this book is that uncovering the root causes of problems is good, but blame, which is largely an emotion-laden accusation, is non-productive and harmful. People often get confused by this distinction, thinking that if bad things happened and they know the exact cause, then blame is appropriate.

For instance, a week prior to my writing these words, an important presentation was being made to a board of directors by the new chief operating officer (COO) of a company. After the presentation, when board members wanted some follow-up information, the presenter was unable to answer basic-sounding questions. All the board members quite naturally concluded the new COO was inept. The gentleman left the room at the end of the question period. Looking for blame, when the board members were alone with the CEO of the company, they immediately revealed their assessment that the CEO had made a terrible mistake hiring the man.

Over the next week I learned that all of the judgments turned out to be incorrect and were a colossal waste of time. The COO had been unprepared for the questions (for reasons I won't belabour) and was embarrassed and deflated because he could feel the judgments made by the board members when he was unable to respond to their questions intelligently. The board members reached incorrect conclusions about the appropriateness of the CEO's choice of COO, and, as of this moment of writing, they're harbouring incorrect opinions. The CEO is angry with a bunch of other people that circumstances have come to this. So, in effect, all these conclusions, feelings, judgments, defences, partial communications, and awkwardness are incorrect; they're also harmful and time-wasting.

Scientists have looked inside the brains of people engaged in blame and have discovered it isn't just a rational process undertaken by the purely intellectual, analytical portion of the brain; indeed, it also incorporates signals from the limbic system, meaning there's an emotional element to blame.[1] So we might think blame is a rational process of attributing cause so that we can avoid a problem's recurrence, but it carries with it an evaluative thread that infects a culture with emotional charges that are caustic to organizational health.

But surely, you might argue, there's nothing wrong with getting frustrated with a presenter who can't answer basic questions; after all, this natural cause-and-effect dynamic — a man chose to speak on something he knew nothing about and he should be blamed for his choice — actually takes us to a better place, as long as we hold the man accountable, right? Well, not so fast.

In this case, as in all cases, the effect of a propensity to blame is to make the COO feel small, less able to do his job with a clear head. He might take a different approach in the future, but it will be because of fear rather than choice. The fear could demotivate him and make him resentful, less creative, and less productive. The community of people that participates in blame gets its eyes taken off the ball and is more inclined to cultivate greater blame in the organization. And the bosses (the CEO and the board members) who reinforce the blame culture can get entangled in their angst while they're trying to make the right decisions about things.

The negative emotional pollution emitted in a blame environment correlates with, if not mirrors, the experiences of people with low self-esteem. These reactions are proportionate with the frequency, intensity, and duration of blame bouts:

- feelings of helplessness
- passivity
- loss of control
- pessimism
- negative thinking
- strong feelings of guilt, shame, and remorse
- reduced creativity
- risk aversion

In a healthy culture of accountability, the blame game doesn't get played and all of the above pernicious effects are avoided. Instead, back to our example, board members adopt a nonthreatening stance with the CEO regarding what went wrong concerning the COO's inability to answer questions — they ask about it, for sure, but it's all in the asking. Also, in a healthier environment, the CEO would be less inclined to defend and more inclined to calmly tell the board members that their curiosity is understandable but easily cleared up. All this would add up to less angst and wasted time and more productivity.

> The negative emotional pollution emitted in a blame environment correlates with, if not mirrors, the experiences of people with low self-esteem.

FALLACY OF THE SINGLE CAUSE

People often think one main thing can be blamed for a misfortune, but that's not the case. Usually there are many factors involved. Here's an example. A person I know is usually late for pretty much everything unless she perceives it as very important to her. She doesn't really even acknowledge, when she breaches a promised arrival time for a meeting, that she hasn't actually lived up to her word. Her view is that things happen and that people need to be flexible to survive in this world. While I readily acknowledge her wisdom when it comes to things like work–life balance, I still think if she says she'll be there at 10:00 a.m., she should indeed either arrive on time or let folks know of her tardiness.

Last month was another occasion of the same nature, only this time there was a hard deadline or an opportunity would be lost. It was to submit a final document for a request for proposal (RFP) — usually a relatively rigorous process, the rules of which must be followed by all participating. Due to her lateness, her contribution to the document had to be omitted. Her company lost the opportunity, even though it had submitted its (incomplete) document on time. Everybody on her team blames her for the significant loss. She, on the other hand, blames the lube job technician who was late doing work on her car. She swears that for this particular meeting she was making a distinct effort to honour the deadline. "After all," she said, "I wanted the business, too!"

> People are so eager to put a finger on what went wrong that they're quick to blame the biggest factor and be done with it.

But what are the other factors involved in the company's lost bid? Well, aside from the fact that the submission didn't contain the tardy employee's content, the business opportunity was won by a vendor who, it turns out, was secretly preferred by the buyer. Also, her company's product wasn't competitively positioned in the marketplace. You get the idea: people blamed the late person, even though a variety of other factors was at play.

Psychologists refer to this mistake in critical thinking as the "fallacy of single cause." People are so eager to put a finger on what went wrong that they're quick to blame the biggest factor and be done with it.

THE TRUTH OF THE MATTER

So, when bad things happen, who *should* we "blame"? Or, more precisely, or even just to avoid the word *blame* altogether, since it's so loaded with baggage, how ought rational people enumerate the factors involved in any given failure? The following questions can be asked to get the ball rolling:

1. What cultural factors (in our organization, family, relationship) create a context for this matter?
2. Where was the initial slip-up?
3. What things could have been done in order to prevent this slip-up?
4. Who had the earliest chance to prevent it? Who had the last chance to do so?
5. Who were all the people who touched or were connected with the problem, and what role did each person play in the problem?
6. What could those people have done differently to catch the problem and prevent it?
7. Who could have caught this before it happened?
8. What could be done to avoid this from recurring?
9. What role did I play in this problem?
10. What could I have done differently?

When the above questions were explored by the "guilty" party and her colleagues discussed above, they arrived at some deeper and more productive discoveries. They agreed they had a regrettable, culture-wide history of condoning lateness and other non-productive behaviours and installed measures to limit that behaviour. In the case of our friend who was "always" late, she agreed she would resign if she didn't comply with a new set of standards that she helped construct. But they also revisited their procedures for handling RFPs. Furthermore, they concluded from this experience that their sales team needed to get much closer to customers to know what they liked and disliked about the organization. This list goes on, of course, but the point is that the initial blame was ill-founded.

> Uncovering the root causes of problems is good, but blame, which is largely an emotion-laden accusation, is non-productive and harmful.

BLAMING OTHERS

Why do people leap to blame? There are several answers to this, including the following:

1. Sometimes blame is a place to put our anger and pain, sort of like a steam valve — the energy builds, and it discharges through blame.

2.   Blaming others is a handy way to deflect personal culpability. This is especially true for people who have spent years defending themselves from painful accusations. When something goes wrong, they safely and quickly declare, "It wasn't me!"

3.   Blame can make us feel that things are under control; we feel that if we can answer the question, "How did this happen?" we know what's happening.

4.   Blame can be a tool for revenge; usually expressing resentment for some perceived past wrongdoing, the blamer seeks to hold others accountable. Many people find that vengeance feels good.

5.   Blame can make us feel superior to the person being blamed.

Essentially, blame is an ego response, not coming from the centred sense of self where, for example, our willpower resides, but from a part of us that sees itself as up against, underneath, or above something or someone.[2] The impulse to blame takes us away from a place of relative peace and puts us in a mental space of narrowly focusing on and identifying with any one of the motives mentioned above. Blame is usually informed by strong feelings and transmits to others — the person being blamed and others who are privy to the accusation — a sense of judgment. This judgment is poison to a culture of account-ability. It is a bit ironic because many of us feel that finally achieving a culture of account-ability means finally making people admit to their failures. But the essence of a full-fledged community of people who are accountable is actually about each individual in the community "unfolding" toward greater and greater self-responsibility. To encourage this culture, leaders must judge behaviour but not people.

> Essentially, blame is an ego response, coming from a part of us that sees itself as up against, underneath, or above something or someone.

Leaders and others who want to get out of the habit of projecting judgment when they would really prefer to unpack what went wrong and move toward productive change can consider the following approaches:

1.   Take a breath before you attribute cause. Buy some time to gain your composure.

2.   Seek to get the facts rather than cite your hypothesis.

3. Avoid appearing to be on a witch hunt. You can even say, "I'm not looking for who to blame in this situation, but I do want to understand."

4. Send signals that you value mistakes because that's how we learn, and don't hesitate to highlight that even someone who knows better is undoubtedly still learning, still growing.

5. Instead of "I can't believe you" or "You should have," try "I want to understand what went wrong" or "Help me understand how."

SILOS, DEPARTMENTAL ACCUSATIONS, AND UNENDING WARS

Having one person who tends to blame others on the team is tough enough, but working in an environment where blame runs rampant is almost torturous. Even worse are situations in which two departments are ostensibly at war with each other, with all the individuals from both communities participating in accusations and resentment. Sometimes this happens because the leaders of the groups in question haven't resolved their own relationship issues. As a result, they act as role models for their underlings and contribute to the creation of one big blame game. Other times a senior leader responsible for both teams unwittingly and excessively energizes both sides of what would otherwise be a healthy, organic core polarity. Such healthy polarities abound in organizations; they show up as the checks and balances that help organizations move toward their goals. But they also create a context for interdepartmental blame.

A common example is the tension between sales and marketing teams, the former believing that the latter group doesn't understand what's happening in the real world, and the marketing people thinking that the sales force isn't strategic enough. Similarly, sales and operations teams go into conflict, with operations people feeling that sales people are making promises that can't be kept, while the sales team believes that operations personnel don't understand that the heart of the business is in selling to customers and selling requires more optimism than realism.

And then there is the predictable tension between people who are accountable for saying no at the right times to people whose job it is to get them to say yes. Banks, for example, want to loan out as much money as possible, while their credit approval departments are the naysayers, seeking to mitigate risks.

The point is that polarities are built right into most corporate systems, and it's the job of leaders to find common ground, synthesizing the best of both worlds. They need to act as role models for non-defensiveness, to fashion a non-judgmental approach to assessing where things have gone wrong, opening up lines of communication, seeing the slings and arrows of life in the other group's trenches, and educating all the players on the interconnectedness of their individual and departmental roles. It takes basic, sustained mental health for leaders to effectively work within these natural polarities, and we'll explore this in more depth in Chapter 8, "Being the Boss."

> Polarities are built right into most corporate systems, and it's the job of leaders to find common ground, synthesizing the best of both worlds.

Blame is one thread in the fabric of tensions such as this. Another thread is defensiveness, the effort to defend against it.

DEFENSIVE PEOPLE

With blame, and the fear of blame, comes the common but not necessarily inevitable effort to defend against it. Another ego manifestation, defensiveness is one more obstacle on the path to accountability, and it's the opposite of full personal responsibility.

Most people who tend toward defensiveness are quite disinclined to admit it. When you tell them they're being defensive, they usually reply with, "No, I'm not." It's a somewhat impenetrable circularity built right into the defensive way of being. People become defensive not just to be difficult but also because they perceive a threat either in a specific situation (such as being proven wrong on a certain matter) or, more deeply, pertaining to their sense of personal value, workplace security, career aspirations, or level of authority. People who tend to be defensive usually think it's situation-specific, when it's actually the deeper fear being provoked.

> People become defensive because they perceive a threat in a specific situation or, more deeply, pertaining to their sense of personal value, workplace security, career aspirations, or level of authority.

For example, if you work with someone who's defensive and you want that person to overcome the tendency, try to get to the bottom of the perceived threat and help him or her overcome it. Sometimes just getting someone to say something like, "Yes, I'm afraid for my job," or "I suppose I'm afraid of not getting a positive performance rating," or "I want that next promotion," or "I acknowledge that I'm in a power struggle with you" can relieve the pressure that elicits the patterned response. My experience is that, for really tough cases of defensiveness, it's necessary to at least get people to acknowledge that, even if they're not defensive, there at least is an optics issue such that they're *perceived* to be defensive. This generally opens them up for a look at what non-defensive behaviours they can exhibit to address the optics. It doesn't take them all the way to "clear," but to call upon an old adage, sometimes if you whistle while you work, you end up being happier about it.

IF YOU ARE DEFENSIVE

If you know you personally tend to get a bit defensive, you probably know that it doesn't look good on you; it can harm relationships, and it certainly isn't conducive to full self-responsibility. It can also rob you of time when you feel encumbered by stirred-up feelings.

Sure, sometimes people's accusations and implied accusations can be unfounded, and you owe it to yourself to clarify for people. And sometimes, practically thinking, you have to pretty much fight others in order to clarify, lest they hold some unfair opinion of you and other more long-term consequences are brought to bear. So, of course, do what you have to do. But to get underneath the pattern of defensiveness itself, you might explore why you tend to be provoked. There are likely multiple pieces to the puzzle, and you can assemble them through questions such as these:

1. Are there certain matters about which you find yourself more defensive?
2. Do you generally fear for your job? What is at stake if you're found negligent in some way?
3. What does the feeling of being blamed remind you of?
4. What is the role of those memories in your robotic response nowadays?

Usually, there's a chain of logic at play, and at the end of the chain is one of the deepest fears of all: feeling so small that you almost disappear. Put another way, deep down, most of the defensive people I've tried to help over the years use defence against blame to deal with a fear of having no value or, basically, of being zeroed out. Sometimes at the end of the chain of logic is a deeply embedded memory of actually feeling really, really small, the way a child would feel during punishment. The adult's faint memory of the experience fuels the defensive machine in adult life. Other times at the end of the chain of logic is a mistaken, very private belief that we're essentially worthless. Any evidence other people bring that might support the hypothesis gets counter-argued, because, if true, it would be as bad as the end of life itself.

Of course, both of these scenarios are absolute illusions. In fact, finding self-responsibility is all about tapping into a progressively growing sense of self-worth, self-acceptance, self-love, and self-compassion, and a strong sense of self-efficacy. The idea is that these attributes are at our disposal. They're already in there; it's just that direct access to them is obscured by confusing patterns of thinking, sometimes exacerbated by the culture in which we live and work. A blame culture, for example, is obviously unhealthy for anybody on a mission to get past defensiveness. A judgmental boss is anathema to personal unfolding. Being surrounded by unfairness, forced into untrusting relationships, working in a totally unpredictable environment, being looked upon as inferior — these are all the polar opposites of what we're looking for here.

Here's an example of the logic chain we can use to work backward from a bout of defensiveness to an individual fear of low self-worth. It comes from a real-life dialogue. The following is a list of answers to questions about a specific incident. You can probably infer the questions from the nature of the answers.

1. I got blamed for not following the protocol.
2. I wasn't able to follow the protocol.
3. The protocol didn't allow for realistic exceptions.
4. He said I'm always breaking the rules.
5. The implication is that I'm neither respected nor even liked.
6. If I'm not respected, then it would hurt.
7. It would hurt because I want to be liked.
8. If I'm not liked, then I'll be alone.
9. If I'm alone, I would feel small.
10. I hate to feel that small.
11. I can see how I'm defending myself in order to avoid feeling that small.

The cathartic line of questioning that would follow the above logic chain explores whether the person can see how the fear of being small is inside the motivation to defend. That's usually a moment of big discovery.

Escaping from or avoiding defensive behaviour in the future takes self-awareness and practice. It takes place either during or after an episode and involves the person

1. recognizing the defensive behaviour;
2. labelling it (such as "There I go again");
3. saying to oneself, "This is driven by my deep fear of not being okay"; and
4. not being that child inside and saying, "I am the adult and quite capable of owning and correcting this situation."

The last item above is obviously more easily read than executed, because sometimes a part of us actually believes we are, at the core, unacceptable. That, too, is an illusion, but it's very difficult to overcome.

Candidly, my experience is that the best practical tool to overcome such a mental paradigm is to practise overriding our self-talk to counter the belief. Here's an example of something I've seen that's been highly productive in several cases: "I accept myself fully and completely, even when I make mistakes." The meaning of those words is initially counterintuitive because it runs contrary to private, unspoken feelings. But if the sentence is repeated 20 or 30 times, we can experience a surprising shift in outlook. You have to "make yourself mean it" (as in, try to mean the words). It's not a magical spell we're talking about here; it's a way for one part of the brain to override the premises of another area of the brain.

> My experience is that the best practical tool to overcome the lack of self-acceptance that can lead to defensiveness is to practise overriding our self-talk to counter the belief.

The most profound aspect of all this is that defensive people, or for that matter all those who experience shame, are being invited to accept themselves despite what they or anybody else has to say. In other words, even *if* I made this mistake or that, or got caught speeding, or talked back to the boss, or committed some other dastardly sin (to a limit, of course), I'm still worthy of self-love. There's a little person inside each of us who just wants to be heard, valued, and nurtured.

This takes us back to the topic of blame and how to deal with the little person who resides inside the blamer and wants to be heard. The dynamic is the same. For some reason the person who's allocating blame feels that an assault of some sort has occurred, and the person doesn't want to be shut down or ignored; the person wants to be acknowledged. The polarization implied in the tension between a blamer and a "blamee" is highly unproductive. Obviously, in this book I'm promoting the idea that the blamer needs to rise above the emotional attribution of culpability and stay focused on specifics, rather than judge the person or ascribe an intent to which he or she has no real access.

Let's now consider what the blamee can do to defuse the blamer's electric charge. We can start with some assumptions:

1. The blamee needs to approach the situation with a sense of his or her own self-respect and self-worth. Regardless of guilt or innocence, we don't want the interaction to be between the blamer, someone who, by our definition, is tapping into the brain's emotion centre, and the similarly non-centred blamee. In the language of transactional analysis theory, we don't want a child-to-child interaction.[3] At the very least we want the blamee to approach from an adult point of view.

2. The blamee needs to give the ego of the other person the feeling of being heard. This can be the toughest part of all, particularly if the blamee believes him- or herself innocent of all charges. How can you make someone feel genuinely heard when the person is blaming you for something you didn't do? Sure, we apologize if we're flat-out wrong, but usually we're in a grey area, such that we played at least a secondary role in the blamer's situation. The idea is that out of our genuine desire to maintain healthy relationships, we need to own up to the impact we've had on that person, guilty of the exact charges or not.

So let's address the notion of apologizing as a social tool for optimizing relations with others.

DOES THERE NEED TO BE AN APOLOGY?

Some people take the stance that they rarely need to apologize because, when it comes to other people, they rarely do anything wrong. Sure, the people around them sometimes take offence at things, but it's not because of any wrongdoing — it's because the offended parties misunderstood or have their own baggage or vulnerability.

I coached a person with this point of view. He's a very smart, successful leader who is somewhat disliked by co-workers because some of them perceive him as cold and maybe a bit condescending. Here's a small example of the type of trouble he would find himself in. One day, in front of others, he said to a stressed-out colleague, "You should probably chill out. Your employees are getting jumpy."

The colleague replied to my client, "You're in no position to know what's in my head, or how I feel, or even to give advice on how I ought to lead my team!"

The next day another colleague explained to my client that an apology was probably due. "You were somewhat invalidating with your comment," she said. "It caused hurt feelings and brought no value. I think it would be smart to apologize."

My client had no interest in apologizing. His position was that he did nothing wrong. He explained that he certainly didn't feel any guilt and that he was actually trying to help. The notion of apologizing for the sake of the relationship was distasteful to him. But he was certainly willing to talk it through with the hurt colleague. In that "talking it through" conversation, he did offer, "I'm sorry your feelings got hurt."

> Apologizing means embracing in yourself the idea that you have the power to hurt people and are responsible enough not to exploit it.

This was met with, "That's not an apology. That's not you taking responsibility for your insensitivity. It's just a way of sidestepping personal responsibility. You said what you said, and it was offensive."

Here's the thing. The perception of remorse is pretty important in an apology. The apologizer needs to show that he or she *feels* some kind of regret. In fact, generally speaking, the more feelings of regret that are revealed, the more effective the apology. Forgiveness comes from the apologizer owning or taking full responsibility for the sin.

But what if the alleged offender doesn't feel that any wrongdoing occurred, or feel any remorse whatsoever? Apologizing means embracing in yourself the idea that you have the power to hurt people and are responsible enough not to exploit it. It's not necessarily about feeling guilty. It can be a simple acknowledgement of responsibility. Apologizing means you care that the other person is hurt.

I NEVER MEANT TO HURT YOU

Just don't say you never meant to hurt the person. It misses the whole point the other person wants you to hear. This response gets offered by people when you say they did something wrong but they don't really feel they did anything bad.

A person I know said something that was potentially hurtful to me the other day. We were at a coffee shop and both noticed a very overweight woman. The woman had just ordered a non-fat latte. My friend waiting in line with me leaned over and whispered into my ear, "Who's she trying to kid?"

As we walked back to work sipping our drinks, I pointed out that, of course, we had no way of knowing why the obese-looking patron was overweight. "You never know," I said. "Maybe her issue, if she has one at all, isn't related to milk fat. Or maybe it simply doesn't matter to her. Who are we to judge?"

My friend's reply was, "Oh, come on! You know very well what's going on here. Look at you, for example; you've got a paunch, and it obviously comes from one thing only: you take in more calories than you burn."

I changed the subject. In a different conversation the next day, I made a playful reference to her calling me fat. It was something like, "You called me fat!"

She said, "I hope you weren't offended. I didn't mean to offend you."

I made a mental note at that point about writing this section. That was a perfect example of what I would call a pseudo-apology. Maybe a faux apology.

I swear I wasn't really offended; though, admittedly, since I brought it up a day later in conversation, it had obviously hit some kind of soft spot. But it troubles me when people hide their responsibility for what they say behind some description of what they did or didn't intend. It's not about what you intended! It's about the effect that's resulted. Maybe from the blamee's point of view no tangible wrong was committed. But from the universe's perspective, somebody has been provoked, and the blamee, powerful person that he or she is, is in the blamer's sphere.

My colleague correctly said I have a paunch and that pretty much by definition I consume more calories than I expend. True and true. I don't need her to acknowledge a causal relationship between her words and my offence, but I would appreciate an acknowledgement that the meaning of her words correlates in some way with my experience of them. The same goes for my client who suggested his colleague should "chill out" because her employees were getting "jumpy." My client's view was that he was being honest and, despite his glib choice of words, he was giving good advice. What the recipient of the advice wanted to hear was that my client played a role in her becoming upset. He was insensitive to her feelings. He took no responsibility for them. When he finally got his head around the idea from some outside perspective that he did indeed play a role in her distress, he found a way to genuinely say, among other things itemized in the list below, "I'm sorry for my choice of words. They were hurtful and unwarranted."

> Sincere apologizing requires us to shift out of the more narrow-minded defensive posture that usually protects us against feeling small.

Research has shown that effective apologies contain eight elements:

1. Using the words *I'm sorry*
2. Acknowledgement that you erred
3. Explaining how you'll fix the situation
4. Describing what happened, and being sure not to attribute responsibility elsewhere
5. Promising to improve in the exact area of the offence
6. Ensuring the person sees that you know precisely how you hurt or offended him or her
7. Expressing that you were wrong
8. Asking for forgiveness[4]

FORGIVING

Mahatma Gandhi said, "The weak can never forgive; forgiveness is the attribute of the strong."[5] Sincere apologizing requires us to shift out of the more narrow-minded defensive posture that usually protects us against feeling small. And that shift often calls for wisdom, for example, to know that we can rise above a personally felt need to defend; courage to expose ourselves to an accusation that might prove we're culpable and, so, potentially smaller; and clarity to navigate a delicate conversation that could easily degrade into a clash of egos.

> Forgiving often means releasing our tightly held grip on the belief that we've been wronged and moving into a point of view that entertains compassion.

Forgiving also comes with its own challenges. It often means releasing our tightly held grip on the belief that we've been wronged. Sure, if somebody lays out a truly humble apology, then forgiveness becomes easy. The real challenge is in forgiving the person who rejects culpability or who can only vaguely allude to some role in an offence.

Forgiveness means letting go, such that there's no grudge. It requires a blamer to step outside of a perspective that can clearly see a transgression and into a point of view that entertains compassion. And it means staying there. Don't go back in. That's what fuels a blame culture.

Until the transgression recurs ... and recurs. If somebody continues to repeat a behaviour and your forgiveness doesn't feel real to you anymore, the other option is to totally unpack the patterned behaviour in a face-to-face conversation with the person. Perhaps one or both of you will discover something new and valuable. Or not. You always have choices: to limit your time investment, to emotionally exit the dilemma, or to leave the relationship.

MOVING TO A BLAME-FREE CULTURE

Let's collect our thoughts here about how blame is a useless, time-wasting endeavour that is the polar opposite of how self-responsible people act in a culture of genuine accountability:

1. Unfortunately, blame contains a judgmental, evaluative aspect that's poisonous to a culture of people who are becoming more personally responsible. It makes people feel smaller, consumes time, and is usually hurtful. The pain that blame causes can spread like a virus.

2. When a subtext of blame arises in a group of people seeking a culture of full personal responsibility, attention needs to be placed on the multiple contributing factors (rather than on allegations of a single cause), on what can be learned, and on what steps should be taken.

3. When we manage people, we shouldn't set ourselves up as role models for blame. That means we should focus on results, behaviours, and other observable things, rather than on how a person is at fault.

4. We should transmit to others the willingness to take full responsibility for things that go wrong, which will help them see it's okay to make mistakes and be human.

5. If we lead defensive people, we need to know they're afraid of something. Could it be they're afraid of us?

6. If we ourselves tend to blame others or to get defensive, it's good to know what we're afraid of. If it's real, we need a plan to deal with it. If it's a bit of a stretch, or even an illusion, we need to embrace or own that we're okay as we are, that we can deal with what life delivers, and that there might be a part of us that's fearful but we aren't that fear. That is, our centred sense of self, beyond ego, the part from which self-responsibility flows, simply knows better.

7. If we work with people who get defensive, we should help them allay their fear. Acknowledge the parts of what they do or have done that we think are laudable and talk through how things on the problematic matter could change for the future. Understand that inside each of us is a child. That child needs to know that the grown-up *you* will deal with this adult circumstance. The child is okay. Lovable. Valuable. Worthy.

8. If we tend to be defensive, we're smart to learn what beliefs underlie it, overcome those beliefs, and orient ourselves around the overriding stance that we're valuable in our own right, regardless of what others say or what we actually did by mistake.

9. If we're being blamed, we need to own our part in a failure, direct our own and everyone else's attention to what can be learned, and seek solutions. Owning our part in a failure also means finding the courage to apologize. Genuinely offered apologies soothe painful wounds.

6
THE TWELVE OBSTACLES

It makes perfect sense for an organization to seek full internal accountability, because finding it promises control, predictability, efficiency, and maximum performance to achieve time-bound objectives. A tight ship has quite an allure. So leaders want hard-working, dedicated people striving to achieve agreed-upon goals in a predefined fashion. They set objectives, clarify job descriptions, fine-tune compensation plans, track performance, ensure the smooth flow of communication, and educate.

But other than in a strict command-and-control environment, such as a navy vessel, organizations don't work like that. Humanity gets in the way. People have their "stuff." The best way to accommodate the human element in the quest for full accountability is to nurture the self-esteem of team members, invite their genuine commitment, and, generally, adopt a humanistic orientation. Sure, to compete and thrive, organizations need to be driven, highly focused, and extremely effective, but that doesn't preclude the humanistic — it calls for it. That's the main point of this book.

> Increased awareness of our own mental mechanics can help us become more personally accountable.

There indeed is a psychological strategy to getting the best out of people, and a psychological strategy for each of us to get the most out of ourselves. My experience as a coach over the past 30 years tells me that the individual challenges each of us face in becoming more personally accountable are accessible and addressable through increased awareness of our own mental mechanics. Guided reflection can boost our commitment, willpower, job satisfaction, life satisfaction, productivity, and team orientation.

In "Anthem," Leonard Cohen, the late Canadian singer-songwriter, wrote about the crack that's in everything and the light that shines in as a result. I do love that notion. For me it suggests that in my current perspective or frame of mind there is a crack that gives me a glimpse into how I might unfold further. Fortunately or unfortunately, depending on the point of view, being human involves always having yet another crack to peer into, just as soon as we think we've sealed things up. We never reach that perfection, but we become more and more responsible as we reflect and correct.

> Guided reflection can boost our commitment, willpower, job satisfaction, life satisfaction, productivity, and team orientation.

I have come to conclude that there are two big questions that tend to expose the cracks: (1) If I were a bit more personally and generally responsible than I am now, what would I do differently? and (2) What's holding me back? These two questions beg for a comparison between how things *are* and how they *could* be. That comparison takes advantage of a mechanism of assessment that comes built in with the human package. We're born with this human capacity, or burden, depending on how we see it. We don't need to explore here what it is about being self-conscious that yields this propensity, but there is indeed a duality of agency at play that has been discussed and explored by thinkers for centuries.

> There are two big questions that tend to expose the cracks: (1) If I were a bit more personally and generally responsible than I am now, what would I do differently? and (2) What's holding me back?

One of my favourite names for it is the "is-ought dilemma." For example, I was late to see a man last Tuesday. My "is" (the fact that I was late) was different from my "ought" (how I really do think I should be more respectful of my word and of others' time). The nature of the personal obstacle inside my head — the reasons I didn't live by my "ought" — is what we're now about to discuss. Experience as an executive coach has taught me there are at least a dozen categories that can help clarify the nature of some-one's personal obstacle. Here they are:

1. Hazy accountability
2. Fear
3. Negative self-talk

4. Feeling like a victim
5. Self-absorption
6. Wiring
7. Compulsion to care for others
8. Simple overload
9. Feeling conflicted
10. Imposed duties
11. Being enabled by others
12. Distractions and preoccupations

The above list shouldn't be seen as some kind of diagnostic model for labelling somebody's problem. First of all, even though there might be patterns in the person's self-defined problematic behaviour, the obstacle might be situational. For instance, when it comes to my home life, imposed duties are the problem, while at work, doing the right thing might be blocked by simple overload.

Another reason we shouldn't pull just one obstacle from the list and call it our own is that there could easily be multiple factors involved. People who find themselves blocked by a feeling of anger, for example, might be best served by reflecting on additional points of entry: negative self-talk, the extent to which they're self-absorbed, their sense of being a victim, and personal overload. In this way, the list of 12 personal obstacles is really a compilation of explanations to be on the lookout for, since they're so common.

So let's go through the list one item at a time to see how each condition described can hold us back from being who we want to be and to see, at least at a surface level, how the obstacle in question can be resolved. In the next chapter, "Coaching Yourself," we'll probe more deeply into the nuances of exploring personal change, and in Chapter 8, "Being the Boss," we'll look at how a leader can create an environment that advances personal change.

1. HAZY ACCOUNTABILITY

Sometimes we know we're accountable for something, but we don't have the faintest idea how to fulfill that accountability. Sometimes we don't even know what we're accountable for. Both are examples of a lack of clarity concerning our obligations. I asked a client who was an accountant in a large consulting firm what he would do differently if he were more responsible. He said, "I would have conversations with people — themselves and their organizations — to nudge them toward new, bigger, better places." And what was holding him back? "I don't think I have the goods — I don't know what the new, bigger, better places look like."

With further discussion he revealed that although he was officially accountable for moving people along, he didn't think he was smart enough to generate the ideas for the people he needed to nudge. We explored the realm of the ideas he had to generate and in time landed on the fact that there were only eight likely directions he had to take his conversations, given the nature of his work. What looked to him like a matter of limited intelligence turned out to be a lack of knowledge: a short list of possible conversational topics and directions. What was hazy became clear just by aiming his attention at a few simple questions and pushing himself to clarify what was possible.

Actually, we might argue that the first five of the 12 obstacles listed apply to this man. After all, he might have found out that he was merely hazy over what he had to accomplish, but he was also fearful of facing his limitations, muttering to himself about those inadequacies, feeling victimized by the universe over not possessing the goods, and somewhat self-absorbed in his regret. The label for the obstacle isn't as important as the two initial questions that point the way toward self-reflection.

Here's another example of a hazy circumstance — a personal example. I asked myself how I would be different at home if I behaved more responsibly. My answer was that I would pay more attention to my promises. My answer to the question about why I don't pay enough attention — what's holding me back — is that I don't stop to listen to my partner. Sometimes I don't attend to the people around me.

Recently, my wife asked me to move a handy little wine guide from an otherwise tidy kitchen shelf. I had put the guide there while I was in the process of choosing the perfect wine to pair with that night's main dish. When my wife asked me to move the guide, I was sitting at the kitchen table studying a puzzle in the daily newspaper and mumbled, "Sure."

That moment, right there, would be an example of me taking on — agreeing to — a responsibility. I know that at that moment most of my attention was already largely consumed by matters much more interesting to me. I gave my word, let's say, heedlessly.

When she noticed the book in the same spot two days later, I got a bit frustrated with her and moved it while mumbling about how the little things in life sure mean a lot.

It would be a terrible thing if my wife had to take me by the cheek, thumb on one side, index finger on the other side, look me squarely in the eyes to command my attention, pause to punctuate the moment, and ask me to commit to a certain duty. That's certainly what we did to catch our dog's attention and get him to stop barking. And I know that sometimes such a nuisance for a delegator might be what the doctor ordered, were it forgivable in the workplace.

> The more mental bandwidth we dedicate to actually making or absorbing our commitments, the more deeply we register them in our consciousness.

The point is that the more mental bandwidth we dedicate to actually making or absorbing our commitments, the more deeply we register them in our consciousness. In Chapter 9, "Organizational Accountability," we'll talk more about how to use conversation to punctuate individual commitments, and how to tease out the tangled threads of a team member's self-declared blocked position.

2. FEAR

Some of us don't embrace our responsibilities because we're blocked by fear. Here are some examples:

1. A CEO didn't address a significant political conflict in her organization because doing so could have led to her being publicly embarrassed. Her answer to the question about what she would do differently was that she would have the difficult conversations. Her answer to the second question was that she was afraid of outcomes. Her solution was to take baby steps toward exposing issues so that she could exercise methodical damage control through a gradual resolution of conflict.

2. A department head didn't address a problem because she was afraid

of confrontation. Once the problem was laid out, the solution was to create a script of diplomatic conversation starters.

3. An entrepreneur was afraid to really lean into the question of determining a point of difference for his company because he was afraid of success! Success might mean having to work harder and being in the spotlight. The solution was to worry about one problem at a time, but the knowledge that the obstacle was a fear of success was a relief in and of itself.

4. Because she was afraid of being told no, a salesperson didn't follow up with clients regarding the status of proposals as much as she thought she should. She was emotionally leaning on the *possibility* of proposals bearing fruit as a source of hope and didn't want bad news to smother that. Her self-created solution was to initially ratchet up the number of proposals she issued and to maintain that new flow, such that when one fell out she would be sure to add another. The long-term effect was to reduce the gestation period of her individual opportunities (because she followed up sooner) and to maintain an even flow of new business. She had to work harder, but she cherished the benefit of sustaining an even higher level of hope in her life.

3. NEGATIVE SELF-TALK

During most of our waking hours, we have unspoken thoughts — intuitions, emotions, sensations, perspectives, desires, and daydreams. Some of these thoughts are experienced as words and phrases. It's as if we have an inner monologue running all day long. Psychologists have speculated that this inner monologue, sometimes called self-talk, plays multiple roles: it reveals our judgments (for instance, "Oh, I love that colour!" and "I don't like that person" and "Hit that ball harder, you idiot!"), our intentions (for example, "There's no way I'm doing that"), and our curiosities ("What is this person trying to say to me?").

Self-talk often precedes our behaviour. If you change the self-talk, you might be able to alter the resulting behaviour. For example, when my colleague says to herself or even out loud, "We'll never get that client to agree," she is pretty much quitting before she starts. On the other hand, if she overrode her self-talk, replacing it with something like, "This will be hard to sell, but it's basically rational so there must be a way," her confidence and her chances would improve.

Interestingly, our self-talk doesn't necessarily reflect either our responsible or our irresponsible thinking; often its messaging, whether we're telling ourselves out loud what to do or just going along with the flow of our thoughts, is simply what we've learned through repetition. I know a fellow whose parents taught him the mantra, "Just try as hard as you can; that's all anybody can expect of you." Now that he is an adult, having repeated that mantra thousands of times over the years, that seems to be his approach to things. I know another fellow who observed for 10 years his boss always taking the easiest path to get a job done, even if it meant cutting corners and doing poor work. So, having labelled in his head that "the easiest path is always the best," this fellow is an expert corner cutter. He unwittingly created a counterproductive self-talk pattern.

> Self-talk often precedes our behaviour. If you change the self-talk, you might be able to alter the resulting behaviour.

We would all benefit from the practice of determining if our self-talk is causing us problems, but my experience is that, if it is, at some level the person already knows. He or she would readily answer the question about what greater self-responsibility would look like with, "I would manage my attitude." The person would answer the question about why they don't do that already with something like, "My first reactions usually express resistance, so I'm stuck in a circle."

Below is a table of automatic self-talk phrases that a person might have, followed in the right-hand column by the predictable outcome of each line of thinking. Notice how the initial thoughts always end with the word *so*, such that the thinker is somewhat on a roll in dancing to the unhelpful conclusion. Of course, this isn't to say that in our heads we always use the word *so* — that word is only shown here to highlight how our thoughts transition from premise to unhelpful conclusion.

The word *so* that bridges the premise and the conclusion reveals a crack in thinking. It's being interpreted as "so it follows that I should," whereas that conclusion doesn't really logically follow, since other courses of action are available. Looking into the cracked logic reveals the opportunity for change.

INITIAL THOUGHT	UNHELPFUL CONCLUSION
I'm feeling tired, so…	I will do it when I have more energy.
I don't want to do it right now, so…	maybe tomorrow I'll feel differently.
There's a lot going on right now, so…	this can wait until a more suitable time.
There's a lot of time left before the due date, so…	I don't have to start it right now.
I don't want to do that, so…	maybe later.
There are other things to be done, so…	when those things are done, I will do it.
I work better under pressure, so…	I will leave it until things get charged up a bit.
I'm preoccupied these days, so…	I deserve some space.
Doing this will really stir things up, so…	I don't need that right now.
I hate being told what to do, so…	I will do this when I'm ready.
I don't have what I need, so…	I will wait until I do.

Here is the same table of limiting or negative self-talk phrases with corresponding overriding ones on the right. Notice that the thinker replaces the momentum-building *so* with the direction-changing *but* at the end of the thought to counteract its negative momentum.

INITIAL THOUGHT	PRODUCTIVE STANCE
I'm feeling tired, but…	I can at least make a dent in it right now.
I don't want to do it right now, but…	I might as well get it over with.
There's a lot going on right now, but…	there's always a lot going on. Now's as good a time as ever to do it.
There's a lot of time left before the due date, but…	I can save myself the crunch later.
I don't want to do that, but…	I usually feel better once I get going.
There are other things to be done, but…	just do it!
I work better under pressure, but…	I could do an even better job if I got started.
I'm preoccupied these days, but…	it would be good to get out.
Doing this will really stir things up, but…	that's how change happens.
I hate being told what to do, but…	I'm learning to get over that.
I don't have what I need, but…	I can at least get organized.

This practice of detecting the implied word *so* in our self-talk and overriding it with the word *but* (followed by a new and improved conclusion) is only *one way* to manage self-talk. There are dozens of other thematic approaches, including

- looking out for and questioning universals in our inner speech, such as *everybody, never, nobody,* and *always*;
- blocking strong words in our inner speech, such as *hate* or *must*;
- discontinuing labelling people (such as, "All people who *x* are *y*"); and
- catching ourselves assuming that one particular occurrence is proof of a claim (such as, "That's another example of ..." or "Yep, that proves it!").

The key point is that we can challenge our self-talk. Indeed, we can find the crack and let the light in.

In one sense, the act of self-challenging is what choosing to do the right thing is all about. The exciting thing here is that there is a highly practical way of doing so that is applicable to all efforts to overcome our appetites and robotic reactions. If I want my organization to be more accountable, and that means getting each and every person to be more responsible, it means I want everyone in the organization to be skilled in managing mental reactions so they can choose to say and do the responsible thing.

It's easier said than done. There are many factors that determine how effective one can be at managing self-talk:

- the topic at hand (how provocative it is)
- how deeply entrenched the thinking habits are
- our mood at the time (for example, when we're already emotionally hooked, it's harder to manage our thinking)
- self-esteem
- clarity of thinking
- self-awareness
- whether the self-talk is rational (even the worst of us can easily overrule absolutely wacky thinking)

Self-talk isn't the only entry point into the question of how to align ourselves with what some higher-level sense of self knows to be the best way to operate. We haven't even made it to the middle of the 12 obstacles.

4. FEELING LIKE A VICTIM

Feeling hard done by isn't likely to encourage our best behaviour. Instead, usually a person who admits to feeling that way is more liable to psychologically or physically withdraw for a while or go into revenge mode, either with passive aggression or displaying outright signs of anger.

A client of mine has three partners and feels that even though he has carried his weight with them, they in return have been nothing but selfish. He feels used and unloved. And his pain and resentment are blocking him from being engaged in the partnership. He has taken the passive-aggressive route in this situation and has withdrawn himself from full engagement. Nobody is talking about it; nobody knows who thinks what, but everybody knows there's an issue.

An advertising executive feels that, without warning, his client, a large consumer products company, has out of the blue gone back to the advertising marketplace to see if there's a better advertising agency out there. The company's decision to search for another agency is driven by a new senior leader who has come in to shake things up. The advertising executive feels it isn't fair, given his agency's award-winning performance over the past several years. He feels hard done by. In his case, he's elected a more slash-and-burn strategy, attempting all sorts of counterproductive measures that shouldn't be mentioned here. I haven't asked him yet what the *truly* smart thing to do in this circumstance is (another way to pose our question number one), but my suspicion is he would admit that he would mount the campaign to beat the competition and to clean up the mess he's made during his recent rant. He would agree that what's holding him back is ego: he feels threatened and prefers a tantrum over diplomacy. Once he finishes with the tantrum, he'll be ready to get strategic.

> Victim thinkers, people who feel hard done by in the relatively normal course of life, typically need to process their feelings and, at the right moment, move on.

Victim thinkers, people who feel hard done by in the relatively normal course of life (as opposed to people who have been victims of real, significant, usually physical trauma), typically need to process their feelings and, at the right moment, move on. The question they can pose to themselves, or that others can ask them, is, "Okay, realistically, what are you going to do about it?" At that right moment referred to above, they'll finally answer. If the answer isn't the equivalent of "climb back on the horse and take steps to make things better," then the time might still not be right.

5. SELF-ABSORPTION

In a culture of accountability in which people are stretching to contribute to something bigger than themselves, egocentricity is like excessive weight on an aircraft that renders it barely able to take off, let alone climb. Although self-absorption comes in degrees, the basic motive of self-absorbed people is to satisfy their own cravings, which usually include getting the attention of others, getting what they want even at the expense of others, and doing what they want because it feels good as opposed to necessarily bringing value to others or to the whole.

> Self-orientation is the opposite of empathy, and empathy is the most important ingredient for building trust, long-term relationships, and team spirit.

Self-orientation is the opposite of empathy, and empathy is the most important ingredient for building trust, long-term relationships, and team spirit. The degree of a person's self-orientation inversely correlates with listening skills, and if a person doesn't listen well, he or she isn't inclined to let a mission's objectives or strategy sink in — not a good limitation to introduce to a community trying to get somewhere.

For our purposes, self-absorption or egocentricity come in three forms: when people see themselves as above others; when they see themselves as below others; and when they regard themselves as up against others. The "condition" is often situational, such that their egos get engaged based on certain triggers. For some people, it's a sustained way of being. When people find themselves believing they're above others (that is, they've been provoked, or they generally see themselves this way), the question "If you were a more responsible person, what would you do differently?" never quite lands well. But most self-report that if they could be better than they are now, they would improve their listening skills. Here is a list of what nine self-absorbed people I discussed the topic with said in response to the question about what holds them back from being a better listener:

1.   My general disrespect for the people I have to listen to holds me back.
2.   My thoughts are faster than everybody else can speak or think.
3.   In truth, I don't care about other people.
4.   People get in my way.
5.   I'm the star of this show; *they're* here for *me*.
6.   I get lost in thinking about how I can use what I'm hearing.
7.   People bore me.
8.   What I want supersedes what I'm hearing.
9.   People don't listen to me, so we're even.

It's difficult for people with this orientation to embrace and execute a commitment to improve. My biggest successes in this mission have been based on helping them connect with their compassion. On the assumption that the vast majority of people are pre-wired for compassion (it has helped the species survive, after all), there are exercises designed to cause someone to listen that go a long way toward personal development.

One of the most delightful, repeated experiences of my career as a corporate educator has come from leadership training sessions I've conducted in which one of those exercises caused attendees to declare the equivalent of "Oh my goodness, I just realized I've never actually listened in my life!" or "My spouse says I never listen, and it turns out to be true! I can't believe it!" or "Wow, that's how you do it!"

The exercise, called the "listening game,"[1] is simple: one person says something to a second person, who has to then tell the first person what he or she heard. The first person is then asked, "Do you feel wholly heard?" If the answer is yes, then they switch roles (the listener takes a turn at being the speaker and vice versa). If the answer is no, then they do it again. Only twice in my career, having trained hundreds of leaders with this exercise, have I seen a person absolutely unable to fulfill the mission. And those were embarrassing moments.

The game sounds easy, but it's not. Here are the things that make it more difficult, in order of progressive difficulty:

1. When the speaker says something complicated
2. When the speaker expresses feelings
3. When the speaker expresses particularly strong feelings
4. When the speaker expresses strong feelings with which the listener has had no personal experience
5. When the speaker says something negative about the listener
6. When the speaker reveals negative emotions toward the listener
7. When the speaker reveals a critical opinion of the listener

After the first one, each of the remaining six categories of things people say to one another is more likely than the previous one to cause a spike in a listener's self-talk, which in turn reduces the ability of the listener to grasp the point. That's because self-talk tends to intrude on communication.[2]

Once they've been dragged through the listening game and have finally nailed what it actually feels like to hear someone, an egocentric person is usually heard to say, "Holy mackerel! I had no idea!" With a revised understanding of how to listen, when they return to the real world, they're more able to undertake the mental processes for authentic listening and make more progress in dialogues. It's an amazing effect. And it's likely to have a long-term impact.

6. WIRING

Many people's minds are wired such that their attention seems to leap from one bright light to another. They're not great at concentrating unless they're particularly interested in the topic. They may intuit what the responsible thing to do is, and they might even agree to do it, but they go off in other directions anyway. The best way to coach people with this challenge is to help them get in touch with what they value highly and to build into their day-to-day lives various enabling devices, such as supportive systems and people, as well as commitment tools designed to keep them on track.

Accountability must come from within, even for people who were born to wander. People with challenges such as these are perfect examples of how systemic solutions to accountability problems don't go quite far enough. The real solution is to facilitate and leverage their free, usually creative spirits. Usually, in response to the question "If you were more responsible, what would you do differently?" these people feel a pang of guilt, since they know that on some level they don't do what their organizations say they ought to do. In response to the question "What's blocking you?" these people respond with, "Rules." In fact, habitually, the systems in place designed to create accountability — ones engineered to keep them on track — are most resisted by people who are seemingly constructed to move from one exciting moment to the next. So there is a kind of angst built right into their traditional organizational life: they're wired to leap, and that's what makes them true to themselves, yet they're led to believe that compliance is necessary to play on the team.

My approach to coaching such individuals is to re-ask the question about what they would do if they were more responsible. The replacement query is "Yes, but what would you *really* do if you were more responsible?" Then they open up with what they really have to offer, and we discover what's holding them back is their job descriptions. That's where the real conversation begins. But even before a revised job description is in order, there are practical, interim steps. As we discussed in Chapter 3, "Commitment," regarding Bernard, who feared he had a mild case of attention deficit disorder, sometimes the answer is to establish support from co-workers, build personal systems to stay on top of what must be done, and initiate personal discipline, as referred to in Chapter 4, "Willpower."

7. COMPULSION TO CARE FOR OTHERS

Many people go so overboard meeting the needs of others they forget to nurture themselves. As a result, they find it difficult to approach some of their more provocative responsibilities in an integrated fashion. I think of people I've coached:

- A 60-year-old sales team leader excessively beats himself up whenever a large sale is lost. His view is that he's responsible for selling to that client, and if the client didn't buy from him, then, by definition, he failed in his duty. He usually seeks a "debriefing meeting" with the client to uncover where he and his team went wrong and, under the heading of "always needing to learn," also conducts an internal meeting to basically see what went wrong. Of course, such inquiries are actually normal and smart because people learn through mistakes. The telltale sign of dysfunction, however, is the angst that comes along with it. Also, he rarely seems to consider that external factors might be at play. His pattern, by the end of this process, is to come down hard on himself with guilt or on others with blame. Usually his lament is "If I had been a better leader, if we'd had things under better control, and if we'd listened better to the client's needs, we would have won this deal," or "If we had our 'stuff' together, we wouldn't lose so many deals." He would declare that being more responsible would mean somehow taking less ownership of the company's and the team's well-being when things go wrong, and what's holding him back is the apparent compulsion to own his team's problem. Needless to say, there are organizational benefits to this person's dedication, but if he perceives his own dedication as going too far, then there will ultimately be negative consequences.

- A woman with three kids who does all the shopping, cooking, cleaning, and nurturing at home is seen by her peers at work to be the most responsible player on the team because she's a workaholic who will never say no to any request to take on more work. After she puts the kids to bed, she returns to her computer by 8:30 or 9:00 p.m. and stays there until, typically, 1:00 or 2:00 a.m., only to get up again at 5:00 a.m. to deal with email and get ready to start a new day. She declares that she would, if she could, manage her compulsion to totally immerse herself in her job at the expense of what she genuinely and deeply wants for her family. Similar to the sales team leader referred to above in this list, this professional doesn't necessarily need to explore the roots of her compulsion but would benefit from answering the question "Yes, but what realistic limitations *could* you set for yourself?"

People who feel compelled to care so deeply are admirable, no doubt, but when they label their obsession as an obstacle to their expression of true personal responsibility, they reveal an opportunity to move closer to what they really want — a way to integrate both loves, rather than one at the expense of the other.

8. SIMPLE OVERLOAD

Unlike people suffering from the above tangle of pouring themselves into, for example, their jobs at the expense of their families, and who come across to others as über-responsible because of the load they carry and how hard they work, some people carry an impossible weight and slip up all over the place. They're simply overloaded with more to do than can be done; they appear to others to be irresponsible, while the real problem is the impossibility of their situation. It's not that they care too deeply about what they've taken on; it's that they don't set limits on what they agree to do.

One client handed me her iPad and asked me to scroll through the list of task notifications as they rolled through multiple screens. All I could say was, "Well, at least you have things under control."

Her reply was to laugh, saying, "But that's just what I've typed out! I have Post-it Notes all over the place, and handwritten lists. And I have a full-time job!" (That point was sarcastic.)

Her initial answer to the question about what she would do if she were more self-responsible was that she would accomplish everything on her lists of things to do at work. Her second try at this question produced this short list: she would learn to set limits, become more efficient, set better expectations, and communicate more. What was holding her back? Simply not having the appropriate words to express limits, not taking the time to list efficiencies she could find if she looked for them, and not knowing how to create expectation-setting and general communications protocols. Needless to say, her employer played a role in this messy situation. As an entity itself, "it" had to admit that being more responsible would mean assigning more resources to these job functions.

9. FEELING CONFLICTED

Sometimes we're so conflicted in our feelings, values, intuitions, and motivations that we're confused and find it hard to be responsible. For example, if my job requires that I fulfill the two opposing objectives of keeping costs low while maximizing quality, at times I might find myself challenged to take a stand I can believe in. I can't own either mission. A colleague of mine explained what happens to her at times like this: "I just sort of go into bewilderment mode and procrastinate."

There are several ways people can address the problem of having conflicting responsibilities, including talking about them to see if the conflict can be resolved. This usually results in discovering creative solutions that fulfill both sides of the conflict. For example, rather than getting stalled on the question of how to maximize quality and minimize costs, a conversation with others might result in a way to quantify things so they know how far they can go on either side, or so they know other criteria for how to decide on difficult cases. I like the simple principle: when in doubt, talk it out.

> Talking about conflicting responsibilities usually results in discovering creative solutions that fulfill both sides of the conflict.

But, indeed, that can be too simple. Sometimes the conflict cuts deeper, such as when a salesperson is absolutely driven to reach sales targets while continually being harassed by operations personnel to follow the rules. This can create an explosive emotional charge that leaves all parties feeling depleted by their frustrations. The best way out of the stalled performance is more than just talk, but through exercises such as the listening game prescribed previously for ego-intense situations.

A kind of cognitive dissonance — wherein someone feels uncomfortable about a conflicting matter such as saying one thing and doing another, and as a result faces everything from trouble sleeping to demotivation — also sets in when a person is charged with two intense and diverse job activities. Also called split focus, this involves, for example, a salesperson who manages the activities of transactions with current customers and also has to generate new customers. In certain industries, the skill sets required for the two functions (nurturing relationships and "pavement pounding" for new relationships) are so significantly distinct that neither one gets fulfilled. In this case, the conflict is more of an organizational problem than a personal one. It's indeed an obstacle to self-responsibility, but the matter needs to be elevated in order to be resolved.

10. IMPOSED DUTIES

We established in Chapter 3 that adopted commitments don't carry much motivational weight; they need to be connected, for instance, to what people really want to do. Making our responsibilities align with desires, skills, interests, and strengths tends to shift a sense of commitment toward what we called the intrinsic side of the commitment continuum. Doing so allows self-responsibility to flow more freely because it comes from within the person rather than as an imposition.

A common thing I see in the business world is people not feeling responsible for a whole array of duties that they never fully bought into in the first place. Their answers to the question about what they would do if they were more personally responsible concerning that array run the gamut:

- I would do what I want to do.
- I would be myself.
- I would change the rules so that people have to be less like robots.
- I would help to find new ways to do things.
- I would fix the way things work around here.

It's hard for people to dedicate themselves wholly to something assigned to them without first getting the opportunity to buy into it. Indeed, autonomy is a prerequisite for a genuine feeling of self-responsibility. Imposed responsibilities might cause the perception of increased accountability in an organization, and usually give senior leaders a greater sense of control, but when those responsibilities aren't linked to what the employee base actually craves, accountability tends to crumble. What a mess!

> Imposed responsibilities might cause the perception of increased accountability in an organization but when they aren't linked to what employees actually crave, accountability tends to crumble.

My firm has served multiple clients who have gone around this bend. One, a large retail chain, was concerned that customer-facing employees (store-level sales and service staff, logistics and delivery personnel, and online chat room hosts) knew their basic jobs, but they were too varied in their approach. There were wild inconsistencies in the culture of individual locations and departments, such that the organization's brand was diffused — customers didn't really know what the organization stood for.

The natural solution that came to mind didn't work. It was for the head office to stipulate relatively minute details of how each job function would operate. Retail store employees were given scripts to guide consumer conversations. Customer service personnel were told exactly what to say in response to each type of customer inquiry and complaint. Drivers were prescribed very specific rules about what they could and couldn't do and say in the presence of customers, and so on. The result of this huge undertaking was indeed that perceived brand consistency numbers dramatically improved. Unfortunately, but not surprisingly, employee satisfaction levels declined due to the depletion of employee autonomy. Also too bad: customers perceived "stiffness" among employees.

Turnover in that industry is relatively high, so rather than go back to the employees to help them process the change they had just undergone, the organization set its sights on the macro problem alone. The ultimate solution, the one that worked, though I'm sure it's a never-ending balancing act, had three components:

1. Slightly increase compensation to make the organization more attractive to higher-level job candidates.
2. Change hiring practices to include measuring a candidate's level of empathy, personal accountability, self-efficacy, and verbal communication skills so the organization could grant autonomy to people who could handle it.
3. Adopt the principle of granting a reasonable level of autonomy. For example, salespeople didn't have to say, "Hi, let me know if I can help you in any way," and within a minute or so, "That's the product I use myself." Instead they had to establish a "quick" sense of attentiveness and accessibility to the customer (through some kind of acknowledgement) and behave in a manner that was neither too intimate nor too distant.

At the individual level, people who feel burdened by imposed duties need to either buy in by finding out for themselves how to make them work or, as crude as it sounds, exit. But the process starts with figuring out how to shift responsibility to the intrinsic side of the continuum. Additionally, finding out how to make things work can include negotiating with themselves or with the entity imposing the duty; visualizing the personal, long- or short-term payback for the investment of will required; strategizing how to cope; improving skills; finding efficiencies; and being very clear on what the commitment entails.

11. BEING ENABLED BY OTHERS

Sometimes other people protect us from facing our responsibilities. Think of the parent who steps in so the child won't have to face the consequences of his or her actions. Or the boss who, upon hearing of an employee who has stirred things up in another department, rises to the employee's defence regardless of what actually occurred. In these cases, the defender has a kind of codependency with the protected person. They play off each other. The irresponsible person gets to run with her impulses, and the protector gets a payback in any one of several forms: the feeling of a tight family or team, control, or keeping her people happy.

> A trap can emerge in an enablement dynamic: enablers get pleasure from handling things for recipients, while recipients don't even have to suffer the consequences of the real obstacle in front of them.

Take someone who finds himself behaving less responsibly than he would like because he's being enabled by someone else. If we asked him what he would do differently if he were more responsible, his answer would sound akin to, "Make my own decisions." The person would attribute what's holding him back from making his own decisions to the person always stepping in.

"But don't you feel protected by this person always coming to your rescue?" we might ask.

The answer would be, "Yes, and that's fine, but I would like more independence."

If you're the person who's been enabled and you would like to exhibit more independence, it helps a lot to ask for it. Show an eagerness to learn, particularly because the person who's been enabling you might be on to something regarding your readiness — he might not think you're ready, for instance.

Interestingly, a trap can emerge in an enablement dynamic such that enablers get pleasure from handling things for recipients, while recipients don't even have to suffer the consequences of the real obstacle in front of them. So the enablement is a block to uncovering the block, if you will. One has to dig a bit deeper to get down to the root causes. It's hard for "enablees" to step out of this addictive game. My experience is that an exercise relying on the thinking explained in Chapter 4 in the section called "I Am Not My Appetites" would help, wherein the enablee sees that "I'm not this little girl who needs Mommy to come to the rescue" and can visualize herself as a fully grown adult willing her way past the enabling dynamic.

If you're the leader of the person who's been over-enabled, pulling back the support requires ample communication (probably linked to "It's time for you to handle things more on your own"). Empowering over-enabled people usually takes a deliberate plan and gradual education. As usual with the obstacles in this chapter, it starts with conversation.

12. DISTRACTIONS AND PREOCCUPATIONS

Some people who are asked how they would act if they were even more personally and generally responsible simply want some of their stresses removed from their circumstances. Usually the stressful matters pertain to money, health, and general life security — things right at the bottom of Maslow's hierarchy of needs (survival-related). Here are some examples:

- A business owner who can't perform her regular job duties because she's so preoccupied with financial matters that threaten the existence of the entire enterprise
- Any person waiting for the results of a significant medical test or anticipating a life-threatening medical issue for himself or a loved one to resolve itself
- An employee base that knows a big shakeup is coming that could have an impact on job security

Why do these things affect how responsibly people might behave? In most cases, people know what they ought to do about the array of day-to-day issues facing them, but they find themselves putting those issues in abeyance until things become secure. What should preoccupied people do? My experience is that they're best off when they're

1. given a voice to articulate feelings and emotions;
2. encouraged to stay busy;
3. staying as organized as possible about only the day-to-day issues and delegating the secondary ones;

4. filling personal time with distraction (to distract from the distraction, if you will);
5. leaning on a personal network of trusted friends and colleagues; and
6. doing whatever is possible concerning the main problem itself (action steps can give a feeling of control, while a deer-in-the headlights reaction can be counterproductive).

KNOW THIS

At the beginning of this chapter we referred to what a certain behaviour or approach of ours *is* versus what we think that behaviour *ought* to be, but there are a few other things to keep in mind.

This book is only about our *own* sense of *ought* as opposed to somebody else's. We haven't talked about where the sense of *ought* comes from, but the assumption is that it's from *you* (your centred sense of self) as opposed to, for example, some robotic, preprogrammed, shame-based sense of morality or peer pressure. Nor have we discussed how to assess our sense of *ought*. Is it rational? Too demanding? Being influenced by nefarious sources? Instead, we're assuming you're the determiner of which *oughts* you want to comply with. We're also assuming, fairly safely, I think, that there's a little room for each of us to stretch in order to get closer to what our true sense of self prefers. That's specifically our mission here.

> Each of us is the determiner of which *oughts* we want to comply with — there's a little room for us to stretch in order to get closer to what our true sense of self prefers.

For example, if you told a little lie, you'd probably wish you hadn't. That's good. If you put off doing what you know is good for you, well, you'd probably want to try harder next time. It's up to you, but this book is partly about how you might approach that. If you're letting yourself down in some way, we've been talking about climbing back on the horse. More specifically, let us allow these basic tenets. If you're

1. unclear about an accountability, it's probably good to get clear rather than stay in the dark;
2. reluctant to act because of fear, it's probably prudent to get to the

bottom of it, because it might be holding you back from the bigger and better things that are right around the corner;

3. suspecting the attitude you bring to your life (job, home, et cetera) is holding you back, challenge the things you say to yourself;

4. finding yourself hard done by, deliberately process your emotions so you can minimize the damage to your life's momentum and move on with a plan;

5. aware you have a big ego that people complain invades your ability to listen, and listening better will help you get to where you want to go, then deal with at least that;

6. wired with attention deficit disorder, consider compensating for it on purpose (building discipline, establishing supports, aligning your job around your operating style);

7. feeling overwhelmingly responsible for every aspect of a certain matter (your job, your family) to the point of hurting other areas of your life, then seek improved, measurable balance;

8. overloaded with things to do, get real and talk it through, off-load, prioritize, or delegate;

9. conflicted, get to the bottom of it rather than shutting down;

10. responsible for duties you don't totally embrace, don't just put up with it. Find a way to connect emotionally to those duties, change the duties, or cut a deal with yourself or someone else to handle the duties;

11. enabled by others and suspect that's blocking your growth, they might be making things too easy for you. Remember that autonomy helps you grow, so negotiate for it; and

12. preoccupied, there are things you can do to cope.

In fact, we've been assuming, as described in Chapter 4, that *you* are your centred sense of self, the part that sees the bigger picture of your world; it's your appetites and programming, such as those referred to in this chapter, that tug you away from your path.

Your path and your pace are up to you. I suggest you light the path with your self-acceptance rather than, for example, shame or the commands of others. We are, after all, discussing the unfolding of your personal sense of being an agent of choice who addresses and overcomes internal, personal obstacles.

7
COACHING YOURSELF

As opposed to helping *other* people become more responsible, this chapter is about *you*. The mission is to reflect on your level of self-satisfaction with regards to being more responsible, and to consider some easy and tangible steps you can take to improve in a manner that suits your purposes.

At my firm's website, www.horn.com, there's a worksheet available to guide you through your personal thinking in this chapter. Hover over the Insights link on the website for a drop-down menu. You'll be able to access a worksheet for your private use.

We'll start with a self-assessment pertaining to ways in which you think you can be more responsible. Then we'll look at a few basic principles of self-coaching and finalize things with a personal action plan.

SELF-ASSESSMENT

Embedded in the self-assessment that follows is a list of all the explored and implied *oughts* in this book so far. For clarity, items that are more nuanced contain extra description.

On a scale of 1 to 5, indicate your level of confidence in the truth of each statement. That is, a 5 means you feel the statement describes you very accurately. A score of 1 means you feel you're a long way from the trait in question.

The items in this assessment refer to your whole life rather than just work or just personal. But if you find yourself a bit stymied by the intuition that your answers would be different depending on which of those two perspectives you're taking, you have a few choices: attempt to average your scores as you proceed through the assessment (which might not be as instructive), adopt one perspective and answer the whole assessment consistently, or download from www.horn.com/insights a version of the assessment targeted specifically at each perspective.

You can ignore for now the five subheadings under which the individual survey items are organized. They'll be relevant when we explore your results.

Responsible (at Work and with Others)

1. I almost always do what I say I'll do, and if I'm going to be late doing it, I reset people's expectations in time. ☐
2. I'm satisfactorily responsive to others' requests for my attention. ☐
3. I readily own my mistakes and explicitly apologize. ☐
4. I resist discussions of blame and instead shift attention to action. ☐
5. To the extent that I'm able, I seek to do my job to the very best of my ability. ☐
6. I'm inclined to participate in solving problems that are in my purview rather than let others solve the problems without my involvement (unless, as a leader, it's my job to delegate solutions). ☐
7. I'm pretty good at doing what I think is the morally right thing. ☐

Responsible (Humanity)

8. I contribute to something bigger than myself; for example, to benefit my community or society at large, or through the quality of my work, how hard I work, or what my organization does. ☐
9. I'm adequately engaged in my society by being up-to-date, engaging in discourse, and voting. ☐

10. I'm pleased with my contribution to the well-being of the planet, in terms of minimizing my personal footprint and maximizing my realistic contribution to the planet. ☐

Self-Responsible (Integrity, Self-Honesty)

11. I act rather than procrastinate when it comes to doing the things I don't usually like to do that happen to be important. ☐

12. I'm inclined to look at where I slipped up and find it relatively easy to acknowledge my slips, at least to myself. ☐

13. I almost always do what I intend to do, even if I don't tell anyone about it. ☐

14. I'm responsible for my feelings, such that if I'm angry or hurt by what someone said or did, I'm aware that I own my discomfort. In that sense, I know the problem is mine. ☐

Self-Responsible (Self-Managing the Day-to-Day and the Future)

15. I ask myself with satisfactory regularity how I'm doing in key areas of my life, then plan and act to adjust my course. ☐

16. I rely on an effective system to keep track of what I intend to do in my personal life. ☐

17. I feel responsible for my mental and physical well-being and invest an appropriate amount of time and effort to maintain or improve both. ☐

18. I have a broad plan to make the best out of my mid- and long-term future circumstances, which includes addressing the needs of those I love. ☐

Self-Responsible (Self-Nurturing)

19. I forgive myself for my mistakes rather than hold on to guilt or shame. ☐

20. I can release myself from taking excessive responsibility for situations I genuinely know aren't really my problem. ☐

21. I nurture myself when I'm feeling low or my feelings are hurt. ☐

22. I'm willing to address awkward feelings I have toward others rather than delay the inevitable or hide. ☐

TOTAL: ____

Interpreting Your Results

The 22 questions in the assessment are divided into five categories:

1. Responsible (at Work and with Others)
2. Responsible (Humanity)
3. Self-Responsible (Integrity, Self-Honesty)
4. Self-Responsible (Self-Managing the Day-to-Day and the Future)
5. Self-Responsible (Self-Nurturing)

Seeing your scores by section might shine a light on a pattern in your responses. For example, do your lowest scores tend to be in one section? Are you surprised by your average score in one section? Do you feel that in one particular section your results would be quite different based on which point of view — home or work — you adopted?

The first two categories pertain to the extent to which you're a "responsible person" in terms of your work environment, interacting with the people around you, and being a member of society. These categories might reflect how others see you since they represent your behaviours rather than how you self-manage your thoughts or feelings. The first category in particular represents what we

> Even with all the systemic tools put in place to create a culture of accountability, the key, often missing, ingredient in an organization is the level of responsibility individuals seem to take for what they're involved in.

called the babysitter mode in Chapter 1, "Responsibility." The idea was that when we engage the services of someone to look after the most prized people in our lives, we seek a person who operates responsibly — exercises sound judgment and chooses to do the right thing. Obviously, a key idea in this book is that this particular way of being responsible is extremely important for an organization that seeks to create a culture of accountability. The idea has been that even with all the systemic tools put in place to create a culture of accountability, the key, often missing, ingredient is the level of responsibility individuals seem to take for what they're involved in.

The last three categories pertain to how you see and take care of yourself; they subdivide the notion of *self-responsibility*. Up to now in this book, we've referred somewhat loosely to that notion, indicating it, too, is a necessary ingredient in order for organizations to be accountable. In other words, we don't just want any babysitter; we want babysitters with self-respect.

COMMON OUTCOMES

Any self-assigned low score on one of the items could present you with lots to think about. But sometimes people's low scores fall into patterns that also might be worth pursuit. Here are five common patterns:

1. **Low on Self-Responsibility:** One set of results of this assessment shows people who do fairly well in the first section — being responsible toward their work and the people around them — while having lower scores in the three self-responsibility sections. Interestingly, while it may look like a pretty good combination for a culture of responsibility, because the final three sections might not be relevant in the workplace, anyway, this isn't optimal. Unless you're attentive to your own needs and are able to look in the mirror and say you're being straight with, as well as kind to, yourself, then in the mid- to long term, self-respect and self-esteem will decline, leading to less of the magic that full commitment and willpower tend to yield. It also implies less creativity, lower job satisfaction, and eventually poor performance on the job.

2. **Random:** Another common outcome is for low scores to be somewhat randomly scattered throughout. Such a scenario usually correlates closely with the obstacles discussed in the previous chapter. For instance, people who scored themselves 4s and 5s on everything except the items that imply they don't seek to do their jobs to the best

of their abilities (5) and they procrastinate on things they don't like to do (11) might readily trace that back to the obstacle called Imposed Duties. Such people just might not be motivated by their job because they can't connect it with what they're genuinely interested in.

3. **A Personal Blame/Defensive Orientation:** This usually shows up via responses to items 4 and 19. It correlates with the obstacles called Feeling Like a Victim and Negative Self-Talk.

4. **Slow Emotional Recovery:** Low scores in items 14, 21, and 22 often go hand in hand, perhaps revealing people who have been knocked a bit off-kilter when, rightly or wrongly, they feel wounded in a relationship. They are disinclined to address the problem, find themselves holding on to their blame or hurt, and might be a bit slow to self-nurture. They can be drawn to the obstacles we called Negative Self-Talk, Fear, and Self-Absorption.

5. **Procrastination:** Relatively low scores in items 1, 11, 13, 16, and 22 can all point to someone who's inclined to procrastinate. Such a pattern might be derived from a panoply of obstacles: Fear, Negative Self-Talk, Wiring, Feeling Conflicted, Imposed Duties, and Being Enabled by Others.

WHAT TO DO WITH YOUR RESULTS

With a sense of which type of responsibility you'd like to get better at, and your knowledge of one or more of the obstacles explored in the previous chapter that might explain what's holding you back, I invite you to take some baby steps toward self-improvement. By the end of this chapter, we'll look at an improvement process that includes

1. choosing which areas of responsibility and which areas of your life to focus on;
2. determining the obstacles that block your forward movement;
3. going just a bit deeper to recognize some conflicting thoughts and cracking through some bad faith that might be hidden in the obstacles;
4. choosing a next step;
5. committing; and
6. closing the loop on executing that next step.

But first there are a few principles to keep in mind. One is the coach's "Prime Directive," the notion of being genuinely non-judgmental with ourselves. Another key principle is that there's no end to this "game" of becoming more responsible: you could ask the most responsible person you know what they would do differently if they were even more responsible, and they would indeed have an answer. The third thing for us to consider before getting down to the process itself is what good self-coaching looks like. Let's examine these three ideas one at a time.

THE COACH'S "PRIME DIRECTIVE"

Here's the good news: just because something has held you back, such as your fear, your essential self-absorbed style, or how you've overfocused on others at your own expense, it doesn't in any way mean you've been dishonourable. Placing your attention on how you haven't been responsible isn't a self-shaming exercise. It's only looking at the cracks in your world view so that you can shine the light in, see what's going on, seal it up, and move on. For sure there will be another crack and another one after that forever and ever — nobody is without a crack.

Coming to grips with the fact that there's nothing wrong with you, nothing worthy of shame, is a starting point in understanding how to coach, even if you're simply coaching yourself. Certainly, from the point of view of the *ought* or the ideal — the intuition that you could be better in a certain way — anything less than ideal is, by definition, inferior. But from an even bigger point of view — let's say, from the point of view of the wisest person in the world, the woman who knows all things, or perhaps the King of Compassion — things are unfolding as they should. In principle each of us is on a path, and we merely want to move ourselves forward at a pace that feels right. Pushing much more than that will yield resistance and is totally unnecessary.

> Genuine accountability is about getting to higher ground, and from that place, encouraging commitment, generating willpower, resisting blame, knowing what has to be done, and doing it.

"But we want accountability now!" perhaps says a voice in the back of your mind upon reading the above paragraph. "Organizational accountability isn't about compassion. It's about people stepping up to the plate immediately and owning what they must do, and darn well doing it well!"

That's a big moment right there. That's the perspective that sucks the air out of the balloon and makes efforts to clean things up land flat. Genuine accountability is about putting things into perspective. It's about getting to higher ground, and from that place, encouraging commitment, generating willpower, resisting blame, knowing what has to be done, and doing it. There's no role for shame.

For example, if you're late every day, what's behind that? Surely, at some level, your heart is in the right place; that's why it's a topic of thought for you (for instance, perhaps you would actually prefer to be an on-time kind of person). Is it because you're exhausted? Unhappy? Frustrated? Resentful? Overloaded? Or is it the bus service? So, as a coach, my (your) job is to get that some part of you wants to be on time and that you're simply blocked. Frankly, even if you're constantly late because you darn well want to be late, that's okay with me, too. Truly. I would just want to know why it's so important to you.

Or if you find yourself quiet at meetings and you believe being more responsible necessitates speaking up, then it will be counterproductive and unrealistic to criticize yourself — find something fundamentally wrong in yourself — for being that way. The question is: what's the obstacle? Your heart, after all — again, because it's *your* topic — is in the right place.

Let's quickly glance through the list of 12 obstacles to look at a non-judgmental stance for each of them. I encourage you to hang your hat on these stances, lest you blow the obstacles themselves out of proportion.

1. Having a hazy sense of what must be done is mostly an invitation to get things clear. There's no need to focus on your irresponsibility for not knowing what you believe in or for what you have to do. The future starts now.

2. Fear is almost always a noble intuition that highlights vulnerability; now step forward by owning the fear and finding ways to be productive despite it.

3. Negative self-talk is inside us for self-protection and it works, sometimes too well; you just have to enhance its specificity.

4. Feeling like a victim is a cry to be heard about a specific matter or even more broadly, but the feeling can indeed be shifted to agency (action orientation).

5. Being self-absorbed only reflects a hunger to be whole; there are other ways to access wholeness. Actually, self-acceptance might be a great place to start.

6. Being wired to prefer freedom of attention is an asset to be respected and leveraged.

7. Compulsion to care is beautiful; the opportunity is to integrate into that disposition a deep caring for the self.

8. Being overloaded is innocent; you're in the best position to strategize a solution.

9. Feeling conflicted reflects good intuition; it's a sign that needs to be read and hopefully marks the beginning of exploration.

10. Imposed duties usually reflect a person's willingness to play along; the next step for you is to find meaning either in the duties or elsewhere.

11. Being enabled was a mistake of theirs; now it's time for you to step up.

12. Distractions are usually more serious matters that remind of us bigger things; you need a deliberate plan to juggle them.

Coaching, whether in the service of others or yourself, calls for a non-judgmental approach.

CONCENTRIC CIRCLES

I see apple pie. I eat it.

If I do nothing beyond satisfying my immediate appetites, I'm not participating in anything bigger than my basest appetites. Yet there's a slightly higher realm I might participate in, one that includes my appetites, and more — my desires. And there's a slightly bigger realm that includes my desires — my thoughts. Bigger still are my dreams of what could be. Attending to each broader realm equates to being a bit more responsible.

> In each dimension of our lives, there is another level up where, if we stepped up to it, we would be more responsible.

Similarly, I see an opportunity to get attention. I take it and make people laugh. If I do nothing but get people's attention, I'm not participating in anything bigger than attention-seeking. Yet there is a slightly bigger, more responsible way for me to spend my time, one that includes getting attention but contains even more: engaging in authentic dialogue. That would be a more responsible thing for me to do.

At work I can be lazy. More responsible activity would include taking the opportunity to be lazy while also getting certain things done. I can focus my attention on the tactical matters staring me in the face, or to be somewhat more strategic, I can put my head up to scan my horizon and think about direction. The idea is that in each dimension of our lives, there is another level up where, if we stepped up to it, we would be more responsible.

So we have the level we're currently operating at, and one level higher always tugging away. And we probably have an infinite number of life dimensions, in each of which we might find such an array of stairs to greater responsibility — always something bigger.

There's no end to it. Don't let anybody tell you they couldn't be more responsible than they currently are, or they don't have an *ought* they haven't fulfilled. Or perhaps they don't like the word *responsible* — no problem. Another treatment of this whole topic could remove the word *responsibility* and replace it with "a bit better, in your opinion, than you already are in any field or life aspect that you wish." *Responsibility* doesn't have to imply weightiness; for me it's about transcending to a personal, higher order of operating.

On a bad day, I'm preoccupied with my micro activities and problems, my appetites, and my robotic responses to the world, but on a good day I open up. If there's enough of me to go around, I step up into those bigger spheres that surround me.

WHAT "GOOD" LOOKS LIKE

The third thing to keep in mind as we embark on self-coaching is what "good" looks like. That is, when you're on a self-coaching roll, progress looks like this:

1.   You break through personal bad faith and are thereby more honest with yourself.
2.   You recognize a pattern in how you handle certain situations and suddenly catch yourself self-correcting before the pattern recurs.
3.   You take responsibility for your slip-ups and your destiny, even for your present moment, so that you find yourself in a position to choose a more responsible approach.

4. You experience self-acceptance, so that when you own your slip-ups, you do so with self-compassion in mind. You're okay as you are, yet you aspire to more. No room for shame.

5. You find yourself experiencing the feelings of "being able" and "being worthy," and they translate into greater willpower, an increased willingness to take healthy risks, and making new connections with people.

6. You develop the habit of including long-term direction in your day-to-day thinking and you modify your choices accordingly.

7. You discover an increased frequency of favourable feedback from others as they notice subtle changes in how you approach things.

PROCESS STEPS

Now that we have a sense of what "good" looks like, let's consider the steps you can take to experience it. The essence of all coaching — whether it's in the context of helping another person or helping yourself — involves choosing what to focus on, recognizing the obstacle blocking the way, exploring it a bit, creating a plan, committing, and checking in on progress. What follows are clarifying remarks and some examples.

Choose Your Soft Spot

As you might guess, self-coaching begins with defining the area you would like to work on. There are several places to start your search. One is to use the results of the self-assessment earlier in this chapter. Perhaps you would like to improve your ability to address awkward feelings in one of your relationships (22 in the assessment). Or you want to overcome your habits that have to do with blame (4 and 19). One of the purposes of the assessment, after all, is to provide some direction on where you might want to grow.

> The essence of all coaching involves choosing what to focus on, recognizing the obstacle blocking the way, exploring it a bit, creating a plan, committing, and checking in on progress.

However, another point of entry into self-coaching is to choose an area in your life and pose the question "In this area, how would I like to be a bit more responsible?" Without much processing, most of us know a spot in our lives where we're a bit shaky. Being a parent? Being a daughter? Taking care of yourself? Your relationship with your boss? Personal fitness? Maintaining your desk?

The process of locating a topic is similar to a goal-setting exercise in which, based on a relatively standard array of arenas, we ask ourselves what could be accomplished in each arena. Those standard arenas are: career, health, family, friendships, personal finance, philanthropic ventures, and spirituality. You could choose one arena and reframe the question around becoming more responsible.

As a coach, I frequently find myself amused when I ask people how they would like to grow or get better. Upon hearing their answers, I pause for a moment and then ask, "Give me another one." They think for a few seconds and then they produce another example. Going through that cycle a few times, they get the sense they've nailed the hottest item of all. However — and this is the interesting part — asking the question one more time tends to produce a response that's even hotter! It's as though somewhere deep in our unconscious are the results of previous unspoken "is-ought" assessments just waiting for the conscious mind to reach in and select them.

What's the Obstacle?

Whatever soft spot you choose, the next question is: what's holding me back? That's where you can either articulate your best answer or go directly to the list of obstacles already explored in the previous chapter. The obstacles might trigger a hypothesis for you, or they might help you to tighten up or characterize your initial answer.

Here are the thoughts of someone we'll call Kevin, who knew about the list of 12 obstacles but simply preferred to avoid the list and, instead, to pursue more independent thought:

> I want to accomplish something in my life. I feel like I'm happy and everything. Nothing is really wrong, but I feel sort of stale. What's holding me back is that I don't have the faintest idea what I want to accomplish. I suppose you could say I'm hazy about it, but I don't even know what I want! I suppose it's that I never really sat down to look at it. Actually, I think it's more that I don't know why I'm here in this world. Like, what is my meaning?

Here are the thoughts of someone we'll call Julia; she wasn't at all familiar with the obstacles:

> I want to become less intense with people when I'm stressed. Sometimes people are afraid of me. What's holding me back is my drive. I just want what I want, and when something is in my way I try to plough right through it, leaving people's hurt feelings in my wake.

Get Underneath It

Often there are multiple thoughts underlying the obstacle, and entwined, they seem to stop us in our tracks. A good step to take in this situation is to label those thoughts. Doing so can loosen things up a bit in order to begin the process of figuring out, in the next step, what little steps can be taken to move things forward. For example, Kevin, from the example above of someone who was stalled in his life because he didn't have a satisfying sense of personal meaning, came up with these simple sentences that were, for him, both simultaneously true: "I feel no meaning. I deeply want a sense of meaning." Julia, struggling to overcome her intensity while stressed, arrived at these simple statements: "I hate people who don't think quickly or strategically. I have affection for my co-workers."

What Can You Do About It?

The next step is to determine what can be done to move things forward just a bit. Usually one's first reaction to this question is "Nothing can be done." Another nudge or two, perhaps with the question "Yes, but if something *could* be done, what would it be?" will usually yield a useful answer. For Kevin, it went like this: "I could find my meaning! I could experiment with different things that might offer meaning. I could ask myself what meaning I would like to adopt." Julia's notion of what she could do was this: "I could assume that getting people to speed up and think bigger requires me to empathize with what they're struggling with before I steer direction." This step of identifying what you can do about the obstacle you've identified is the most important of all. It's what will nudge you from a state of inaction to a tangible next step.

If you know in your heart (or your gut, depending on how you like to approach matters such as this) that your area of growth involves stepping out of a paradigm of putting up with a recurring, private self-dissatisfaction, and you sense that you can do something if you just take the time to figure out what it can be, then I suggest you take that time. Even if you just sit in front of a blank computer screen, fingers at the ready, with the question in mind: what could be done about it? That could make all the difference in the world. For example, the next steps, the baby steps, can be as simple as those listed on the right side of the table below.

THE THING I WANT TO CHANGE	WHAT I CAN DO ABOUT IT
I would like to forgive myself for my mistakes.	• Read a book about shame. • Repeat five times per day, "I fully accept myself even with my mistakes."
I would like to do what I intend to do.	• Use the reminder function in my smartphone.
I would like to exercise, but I always start and stop.	• Join a club with a friend and establish a friendly competition.
I would like to stop participating in blame discussions.	• Get the agreement of someone who shares my desire to stop so we can stop together. • Adopt a blame mantra — "Don't go there" — to block myself.
I want to stop procrastinating over having a particular difficult conversation.	• Start by scheduling the conversation. • Plan a series of bullet points I want to raise. • Anticipate honestly validating the person at the start of the conversation.
I want to stop meandering in conversation.	• Ask friendly colleagues to catch me in the act.

	• Make brief bullets about what I want to say and refer to them in order to keep myself on track.
I want to be more enthused about my work.	• Negotiate some changes in duties.
	• Tell the leader about my career aspirations.
	• Delegate things I don't enjoy.
I want to get my people to be more independent.	• Tell people I'm on a mission to make them more independent of me and start coaching accordingly.
	• Delegate by describing the big-picture parameters and set people free.

The next two steps of the process are pretty self-explanatory. Their purpose is to elevate the personal accountability for execution and results.

What Are You Prepared to Commit To?

This simple step is meant to help people refine their intentions and make them as time-bound as possible. The goal is to answer this simple question: what exactly will you do and by when? Kevin, for instance, could declare to himself, "On Tuesday after work, I'll go home, crack open a beer, and start brainstorming things that inspire me." Julia might promise:

> At my next staff meeting I'm going to explain to people that I'm aware of my periodic intensity and the effect it has on them. I'll apologize and say that the behaviour runs counter to how I actually feel about them. And I'm going to invite people to give me feedback, when the dust of any particular mess has subsided, about how I handled myself. And when they give me the feedback, I promise not to be defensive or explain why I was mad. My goal will be to make them feel heard.

When Will You Check in with Yourself?

This final step in the process attempts to close the loop. It can be as simple as creating a computer alert for a month down the road to remind yourself to revisit the self-coaching process in some way. The key to creating such an alert is to write a note to yourself to explain the importance of paying serious attention to it. Here is the note Kevin wrote to himself:

> You might not feel like this right now, but you know very well that sometimes you do feel empty. To deal with that emptiness, you made a list of things you can do to find more meaning in your life, and that list is below. You promised yourself that on this date you would take further steps on at least one of the list items — a least one baby step to investigate further. Don't just delete this reminder. Please, in honour of me, do as you promised.

Julia's means of closing the loop was to distribute the agenda for her subsequent staff meeting on the day after the meeting referred to above, locking her into revisiting the topic and asking for general feedback.

What is accountability if not acceptance of a closed-loop system that checks in on the progress made against a commitment? Even promises made to ourselves require a willingness to deliberately, thoughtfully reflect on what we've done.

What is accountability if not acceptance of a closed-loop system that checks in on the progress made against a commitment, including promises made to ourselves?

On my company's website at www.horn.com/insights, you'll find the following documents:

1. Self-assessment (as included in this chapter)
2. Self-assessment for work
3. Self-assessment for home
4. Self-coaching personal worksheet

8
BEING THE BOSS

In the context of this book, let's think about the question "What are leaders to do?" A top-line view of what we're talking about shows we want all people in the organization to take more responsibility for what they do (that is, to try hard, do what they say, own their slip-ups, stay the course, and think big). We've said this particular disposition doesn't naturally flow from systems usually installed to create a culture of accountability — those systems support it, but don't create it. It's up to leaders to start the fire and keep it lit. This requires leaders to not just exhibit the characteristics of personal responsibility, but also be champions of accountability who promote and enable the target culture. Such activity makes a "thing" out of the mission, rather than letting the culture simply be the sum of its parts.

> Maintaining a culture of accountability requires leaders to not just exhibit the characteristics of personal responsibility, but also be champions of accountability who promote and enable the target culture.

You might say that creating the culture we're talking about here requires leaders to operate *on* their teams, in addition to *in* their teams or in their bosses' teams. This means that they step back from the day-to-day workings of their realms and think about and act on deliberate plans to nurture accountability. In this chapter, we're going to explore what championing such as this looks like, not in terms of steps to take and communication strategies (those will be addressed in the next chapter, entitled "Organizational Accountability"), but in terms of a leader's daily style of thinking and speaking. We're looking at what a leader can do to create and sustain an optimal environment. First, though, let's do a self-assessment, so we know where we stand and where we're heading.

SELF-ASSESSMENT

This self-assessment pertains to your leadership dispositions, specifically as they relate to some of the key ideas in this chapter, and more broadly as they connect with creating a healthy culture of accountability. The assessment is downloadable at my firm's website at www.horn.com/insights. A version that those who report to you directly can use to assess you is also available at that location (it's written in third person). I'm confident the tools will be very informative and help you to discover the difference between how you see yourself and how your employees see you, as well as help you see how you're doing in creating a culture of genuine accountability.

Indicate for each item a number from 1 to 5 (5 is high) reflecting the extent to which the statement is true of you as a leader, using this scale:

1	2	3	4	5
Not at all	A little bit	Not bad	Pretty good	Exactly

As you can see, a score of 3 on a particular item means "Not bad." There are 25 items.

Facilitator/Enabler

1. I provide opportunities for my direct reports to take on responsibilities outside their normal purview. ☐
2. I provide positive feedback to those who report to me directly on a regular basis. ☐
3. Those who report to me directly perceive my feedback as genuine. ☐
4. I coach and mentor the people on my team regularly so that I'm usually elevating them in some way in their skills and knowledge. ☐
5. I intentionally build skill in my team members before delegating new responsibilities to them. ☐

6. I enable people to work just outside their comfort zones to help them become more autonomous. ☐

7. I empower people on my team by consciously providing gradually less direct support as they take on new responsibilities. ☐

8. I give critical feedback to my employees regularly. ☐

9. I engender a sense that we operate in a culture of continuous improvement, insofar as I talk about how we're all learning, including me. ☐

10. I'm obvious with my team (for example, by talking) about the ways I continue to grow and develop myself. ☐

Humanistic

11. I create a friendly, light work environment for my team. ☐

12. People know they can rely or lean on my steadiness because I'm good at managing my emotional responses. ☐

13. I'm perceived as a genuine person who is respectful of people's time, space, and differences (for example, I don't dominate the room in their presence). ☐

14. Even though it's my job to make judgments, I'm perceived to judge behaviour and results rather than the person. ☐

15. People perceive me as being fair rather than biased. ☐

16. When I give critical feedback to my employees, I do it caringly. ☐

17. People on my team know that I have each of their futures in mind. ☐

18. Unless they're very new to the team, my people feel I know who they are. ☐

Self-Accountable

19. I consistently do what I say I'll do. ☐

20. I'm a good role model of commitment and willpower. ☐

21. I readily own my mistakes without sounding defensive. ☐

22. I hold myself accountable for results, and people know it. ☐
23. I'm perceived to be fussy about details. ☐

Horizon-Focused

24. I deliberately avoid silo-thinking, espousing instead the idea that we (our group and all other groups) are in this together. ☐
25. As much as possible, I keep people apprised of where the team and the organization is heading. ☐

TOTAL: ____

Interpreting Your Results

As indicated above, the best way to take advantage of this assessment tool is to compare your results with the average scores that those who report to you directly give you using the same instrument items. That tool is available at www.horn.com/insights.

Please total your score out of 125. You can assume that if you scored 95 or higher and you did fairly well across the board (as opposed to having low scores in one spot and very high scores elsewhere), your style nicely assists in getting your people to take personal responsibility for what they do. If your score is between 80 and 95, you probably have some soft spots for which you can use this chapter in particular to raise your score. If your score is below 80, you could make more of a mission of reading and digesting all the material in this book. Use the categories described below to focus your attention.

The items in the assessment fall into four broad categories to enable you to spot a pattern in your responses. Those categories are as follows:

- **Facilitator/Enabler:** Items 1 to 10. High scores in this section imply that you've adopted habits that help people learn and evolve in their careers. We'll see in the section entitled "Elevate" that a critical part of the job of leaders is to ensure continuous growth, which focuses attention on what *can* be. And that's part of what taking responsibility is all about.

- **Humanistic:** Items 11 to 18. High scores in this section mean you create an environment that supports self-esteem, one of the most important ingredients in the recipe for taking responsibility. When people feel good about themselves — feel relatively secure (not in terms of job security but in terms of their psychological well-being and safety) — they can afford to come out of their shells and stand up for what personal responsibility entails.
- **Self-Accountable:** Items 19 to 23. High scores in self-accountability suggest you're a role model for what "good" looks like.
- **Horizon-Focused:** Items 24 and 25. Similar to being a facilitator or enabler, as referenced above, leaders suited to creating a genuine culture of accountability are inclined to regularly elevate people's attention so that they see the bigger picture. This takes them out of their local space and provides them with a more global perspective so that, among other things, they know where the proverbial ship is heading.

Let's now unpack several of the concepts referred to above and, along the way, delve a bit deeper into some of the thinking skills required to execute. We'll explore the role of building self-esteem in establishing a genuine culture of accountability, reflect on various ways that a leader can elevate people's attention to the bigger picture, consider how to adopt a non-judgmental view of people, and contemplate being a role model of personal responsibility.

BUILD SELF-ESTEEM

Many leaders have habituated a style of looking for gaps in performance and highlighting them. After all, they think, that's the nature of the game. Fill gaps in performance, and by definition, everything clicks! So they stay focused on the various indicators that tell them how things are going and lose sight of the fact that there are *people*

> With low self-esteem, it's downright painful to take responsibility: in advance of or during a task or job, we feel doomed, and if something goes wrong on a task already done, the psychological threat equates to being spiritually zeroed out altogether.

inside those numbers. Unfortunately, the effect of that over the mid- and long term can deflate the employee base.

The more favourably people evaluate themselves, the more they believe they deserve and are able to achieve their goals. These are the defining beliefs of self-esteem, and they represent the jumping-off point to taking responsibility. In fact, with low self-esteem, it's downright painful to take responsibility: in advance of or during a task or job, we feel doomed, and if something goes wrong on a task already done, the psychological threat equates to being spiritually zeroed out altogether.

Thus, the absolute greatest thing a leader can do to create and nurture a culture of full-fledged accountability is to support the self-esteem of each employee. We know from our discussions of commitment and willpower that people are far more self-responsible and organizationally responsible when they feel they're valued and capable. They're more productive, resilient, diligent, creative, and willing to take acceptable risks. When people feel bigger after they've interacted with you, they have at least a temporary spike in their self-esteem and they, you, and the organization reap all those benefits. When they feel smaller after you're done with them, all those traits go into decline until, after they recover from your influence, they go back to their personal norms in their lives.

There is a virtuous circle in sustaining a culture of self-esteem support, insofar as people who feel good about themselves are more productive, and that personal productivity yields a corresponding boost of those good feelings. The snowball effect does need to be grounded in reality, however, to avoid things like the distracting effects of excessive pride.

There are seven main ways that I know of to build the self-esteem of people.

Positive Feedback

Finding genuine, positive things to say to those who report directly to you, whose work you know intimately, can go a long way to supporting self-esteem. But it's far more challenging to do this effectively than it might seem. We aren't talking about making trite comments or using disingenuous criticism techniques, such as the age-old one of sandwiching the nasty between two compliments. The key is to offer positive feedback in a mindful fashion so the person feels your attention. It takes empathy, the ability to *see* the world from another person's point of view and to *feel* what that person feels. Empathy requires mindfulness — just to slow down and concentrate on those two things.

Let's say there's a fellow on your team whose output is laced with mistakes. You deem the person to be sloppy; you have frequently observed him clicking through a spreadsheet, for example, as if he were a madman; and you've watched the errors occur right in front of your eyes. You just know he's simply going too fast. A part of you wants to jump out of your skin while you yell, "Slow down!"

How can you bring empathy to bear when you feel that way? Indeed, *you* have to slow down and concentrate on *his* point of view and what runs through *his* mind as he does these things. Whether you do it on the spot or later in a relaxed conversation doesn't matter for our purposes; nor are we going to examine how to word the criticism itself. Regarding mustering positive feedback for self-esteem support — and this fellow probably needs exactly that — you need to tap into him. Perhaps you say, "Wow, you really fly!" Or "It strikes me that you really hate to make mistakes." Or "I know hearing me point out mistakes has got to be a real drag." Or "Sometimes I can just see your willpower." Or "We've talked about slowing down, and I know you actually want to do it. Can we talk a bit about what drives you to go so fast — I mean, beyond habit?" The challenge is to know your employees one person at a time.

Some leaders are aware they should offer positive feedback but "forget" to do it. The obstacles outlined in Chapter 6 can help a leader to unpack that problem. For example, leaders can be too self-absorbed to think about patting others on the back, or they can have negative beliefs about giving positive reinforcement that block them from offering such support.

Positivity

When people operate in a friendly environment, they can be themselves and function with a certain lightness in their step. This actually contributes to feelings of being accepted and even valuable (for example, "I'm given the freedom to be myself, which means I'm valued"). On the other hand, raised, caustic voices behind closed doors can measurably reduce the feeling of well-being of those within earshot. Actually, there's a good argument for assuming that it's just plain unprofessional to have loud or intense antagonistic conversations in the workplace (or in the workplace's messaging network).

Positivity can take many forms, including giving high-fives for individual successes and offering compliments freely, but leaders need to be authentic role models rather than feign positivity. Sometimes realists attribute the trappings of unharnessed praise to disingenuousness.

Presence

People get a boost when you're respectful of their time, space, and differences (without highlighting differences), and when you shine light on them rather than yourself. My experience after working with at least hundreds of leaders for over 30 years is that a boss's humble presence engenders a more positive self-image "among the troops" than does a boss's tendency to dominate.

Leveraging Strengths

Within reason, the self-esteem of employees is likely to be higher when they like their jobs. This means leaders obviously have to populate roles with people who are ideally suited to them. Often this is much easier said than done, so that management must confront the question: should we force-fit a person into a role, demanding he or she adapt? Or should we tweak a job description so that we play to a person's strengths? On this particular continuum, assuming responsibilities can be redistributed effectively, I've seen much more long-term success from adapting the job description to suit the person, just to get maximum self-esteem return per employee. The net marginal returns are greater.

Autonomy

When people are allowed to make their own decisions, they develop the belief that they're trusted, able, and free to cause the effects they wish to. Such personal efficacy is a central element of self-esteem. As a champion of a genuinely accountable culture, therefore, hopefully you delegate, not just to reduce your personal load, but also to nurture the sense of autonomy your team members enjoy.

Fairness

People tend to feel small when they sense their environment doesn't support the basic principles of fairness. Cinderella, for example, ultimately unlocked by her magical transformation, had a terrible time until she was valued as an equal with everyone in the organization, including the most senior boss. People's levels of authority and compensation might vary, but they stand as equals on the human stage.

Hope and Predictability

We've already said that the more favourably people evaluate themselves, the more they believe they deserve to, and can, achieve their goals. The efficacy ("I can") element of that formula is the stuff of hope, a pretty well-researched field of psychological needs.[1]

When a leader asserts that there's something tangible to look forward to, something genuinely desirable that's more or less within reach, then hope and self-esteem join to produce confidence, intention, and action. It must be reasonably well-founded hope, of course, or it can backfire. Predictability, or the sense that things will generally unfold as expected, is another behind-the-scenes context that supports our mission here. Together with hope, these elements yield the following types of thoughts:

- I'm worthy.
- I deserve this.
- I'm able to do it.
- There's reason to believe it's on its way.
- I can rely on my understanding of what's unfolding here.
- I'm up for it.

Predictability doesn't have to be pretended. If the leader is pretty good at emotional self-management, for example, people learn to rely on that steadiness. Similarly, even if a future looks rocky, there's confidence in the fact that at least the leader's values are steady. Underneath the desire for predictability is the basic, deep need each of us possesses to feel *safe*. The reliability of leaders and their understanding of what the likely future holds engenders a sense of safety that allows people to open up, take risks, and grow. If people free up the bandwidth that's consumed by worrying, they have more space to be productive.

> When a leader asserts that there's something tangible to look forward to, something genuinely desirable that's more or less within reach, then hope and self-esteem join to produce confidence, intention, and action.

ELEVATE

We said in the last chapter that the next level up from my current world view is the place I should aspire to in order to be a more responsible person or to be more self-responsible. For example, if I've spent years as a basically lazy fellow, but I finally get my arms around why I've been so lazy, begin to learn the joys of being not so lazy, and become more active, then I have a new perspective on things. I see the former view, but somehow I've gotten "bigger." Very nice. You could say I have a broader context on life. I see what I saw before, but I find myself overruling my slovenly ways and choosing to be active. I seem to be operating at a higher level.

Education

One of the jobs of leaders is to enable the people they work with to climb out of their current vantage point and gain a broader perspective. It's a big role and probably one that leaders sort of know about but usually underplay. For example, a good leader grooms her people and elevates them a level in their skills and ability to navigate their environment. That is, she coaches them so they're more effective at their jobs and more able to navigate their careers. This requires the leader to have in mind the employee's current world view and her own world view and to fill the gap as much as possible.

> One of the jobs of leaders is to enable the people they work with to climb out of their current vantage point and gain a broader perspective.

Leaders often make the mistake of telling someone how to do something and assume that with enough repetition the employee will gradually learn to get things right. But they can speed up development substantially if they educate more carefully and consciously. For instance, let's say I work for you and you discover that I once again have created a political mess for myself by being too direct or blunt with folks in other departments. To gain your insight I send you an email that I want to distribute to the other departments and you recognize in this email that I'm doing it again — I'm being too blunt. The least valuable thing you can do is to instruct me in writing to "Try saying it this way …" That would be you making the mistake of assuming that my habitual nastiness will eventually go away by being corrected a lot of times and that this occasion is simply one of those moments. Or it would be you taking the easy way out.

No offence intended. Elevating people is work.

There are many other ways to educate me that would be far more productive in the long run, at least in terms of being educational. For instance, you could say

> First, I do like that you're basically standing your ground. But I still think there are a few edges you could soften. In fact, I suspect you can intuit where they are. I really want us to nail this nuance thing; my incessant pointing it out must be driving you crazy. Anyway, please do have another look and let me review it one more time.

The above involves taking a "boss as coach" approach as opposed to a "boss as controller" one. Our mission is to create a learning environment in which people unfold. As we will see in the next chapter, a culture of accountability leans heavily on the theme that ongoing learning for all is the name of the game: it equalizes (because we're all growing); it puts mistakes into a truer context (and who needs blame in such a context?); it keeps people loose (versatile, open-minded, flexible); it accommodates change (and allows the organization to keep up with a rapidly evolving marketplace); and it develops people's sense of ownership (as in when one proudly declares, "I did that!").

Showing the Big Picture

Another means by which a leader can elevate his people to the next level is by providing ongoing insights into the workings of his own role. Here are some examples:

- Explain where the department or organization is heading.
- Keep each team member apprised of the key challenges other team members (their peers) are dealing with.
- Conduct team meetings to ensure departmental cohesiveness.
- Openly and actively build personal succession plans (for oneself as leader and for each of those who report directly to you).
- Ensure team members are able to respond to significant inquiries from those who report directly to them, other departments, and external entities.
- Perhaps most importantly for our purposes here, speak on a somewhat regular basis with people about how you feel: your full

commitment to the mission; your full personal responsibility for everything you touch; your eagerness to learn and grow personally, professionally, and organizationally; and how you crave those feelings from the people around you. If you give people something to believe in, that they can actually believe in (such as themselves unfolding), they'll move in that direction.

Some Problems Are Permanent

Further to how leaders must offer us wisdom from their higher point of view, there is a profound, subtle skill in recognizing the difference between a pithy business problem and what is really a fine-tuning opportunity *disguised* as a pithy business problem. A genuine, pithy business problem has only one answer. For instance, "Should we hire Judy?" Or "How will we determine which company to buy?" Or "Should we enter this new marketplace — yes or no?" Each of these is an answerable, one-time question to which nobody yet knows the answer. When such a question is answered, it's done. There might be problems down the road, but the question itself has been answered. However, a fine-tuning opportunity *disguised* as a pithy business problem is *presented* as a single problem but is actually just half of a natural, inevitable pair of what seem like opposites. Leaders discern the difference.

Throughout this book we've been referring to the pair of opposites in tension as polarities. An example of a polarity that presents itself as a crisis is "The sales team is once again making promises that we aren't even remotely able to fulfill!" The tension manifesting itself in that lament is the inevitable, ongoing, healthy tug-of-war between optimistic salespeople and realistic operations personnel. Both of their jobs mandate those kinds of thinking, respectively. Sure, fine-tuning is called for, but it's not really a single pithy business problem that has a single answer that will make the problem go away. The problem will never go away if people are doing their jobs.

Essentially, both sides of a polarity are "true," and when one side is slightly out of whack, some fine-tuning is, indeed, in order. But not only are the two sides of a polarity true, they are also interdependent. If we were on a ship, perhaps the most senior leader of all, the captain, would call down to the engine room to ask the engineer to approach a panel of gizmos and make simultaneous adjustments to two dials in particular. Indeed, turning only one dial up or down would throw the ship off-balance.

Polarities can be between departments or within a department. And they can be within a person. Here are five examples:

PROBLEM PRESENTED TO THE LEADER	COMPLAINANT'S SOLUTION	THE "BOTH ARE TRUE" PERSPECTIVE
1. The collections department is getting complaints about being too aggressive with customers.	Tell collections to back off.	We need both persistence and unquestionable decorum.
2. Our production error rates are out of control.	Either stop selling so much or clean up production.	We seek to maximize both quality and volume.
3. This employee is constantly asking for an increase in pay.	I want to tell him to quit if he doesn't like it.	This employee is hard-working and may even be slightly underpaid and the fact is that we can only increase people's pay when we can afford it.
4. This executive who has no authority over me just assumes she can announce what I will do.	This executive should be put in her place.	This executive is making the best decisions for the company and at the same time the people affected by her decisions deserve her full co-operation.
5. We have no controls over who our local managers are hiring, and they're bringing on incompetent people.	We should disallow hiring without head-office approvals.	Local managers need to be agile and bad hires cost us in many ways.

The confident, responsibility-inspiring leader who is addressing a polarity takes the essential position: both sides are true. That is one step up from the common point of view of the normal complainant. Great leaders educate people on polarity management.

JUDGE BUT BE NON-JUDGMENTAL

We've made plenty of references in this book to the paradoxical mandate of leaders: we must make judgments every day, and yet we're also supposed to remain non-judgmental.[2] We've made some references to how that's about judging a person's behaviour and results rather than judging the person, but the use of the root word *judge* does make it confusing.

A quick Web search reveals multiple sites offering a bit of clarity on the matter, suggesting we rephrase the dictum like this: Be discerning, not judgmental. In fact, I would call the most sophisticated leaders I know quite discerning. They see differences and reach conclusions but seem to keep their emotions out of expressing their discernments, and they watch their language and general communication habits.

When others pick up on your emotions concerning the people involved in a matter, they interpret judgment rather than discernment, and it can seriously sour an environment and relationships.

When you discern something about a team member and it bugs you — that is, you have an emotional reaction — you reveal a judgment. And that judgment (the emotional element of it) is likely to push other people's buttons. In fact, some thinkers, starting with Carl Jung, suggest that the fact your own emotions are engaged by an observation you've made or a conclusion you've reached probably reveals more about your own unresolved emotional issues than about the person you've judged.[3] I can't tell you the number of times as a coach I've learned that what bugs people the most about others happens to be the thing they deep down don't like about themselves. The verve they bring to their judgment somehow actually blocks them from being aware of their own guilt or shame or anger about possessing the same trait. Think about it: think of someone, or of a behaviour, that makes you angry and ask yourself whether you possess an attribute that does or used to yield similar behaviour.

In my own case, I can't stand someone employing what I think are influence techniques. If I walk into a store with my eyes on orange peelers and the salesperson says, "That particular model is the orange peeler we use at my house," I think, *Gosh, I hate that — it's so obvious!* A couple of decades ago I came to grips with the fact that I, too, used to employ little influence tactics that were similarly dastardly, and I hated it in myself. Now I work hard to avoid the tricks, but I still can't stand people using them on me.

But that's only one reason our emotions get involved when we make observations and reach conclusions; there are oodles more. The key point for us right now is that when others pick up on your emotions concerning the people involved in the matter, they interpret judgment rather than discernment, and it can seriously sour an environment and relationships. If you yell through the hallways, "Expenses are too high, expenses are too high!" people are going to assume you're in judgment mode. Pretty much anyone you mention it to will feel that you have them in mind as you express yourself.

But people pick up on other signs even if you're unemotional, as well. If your sentences contain generalizations, people infer that somebody is being judged. "That cat *always* walks across my fence." So, too, do sentences containing possessive references: "That neighbour's cat." Sentences that contain pejorative adjectives also do the trick: "That ugly cat." And, of course, you can weave explicit emotionality into the mix and come up with a doozy: "That stupid neighbour's ugly cat always walks on my fence and it makes me sick." That, we could say, sounds somewhat judgmental.

You can discern that it's time to terminate Beluga's employment, and just do it. But don't be judgmental about Beluga. There's nothing wrong with Beluga.

So your job as leader is to send the opposite signal out: that pretty much no matter what, you won't judge. You, in fact, will accept people for who they are, somewhat unconditionally. You discern differences and patterns and you decide. Then the question becomes how you keep emotions out of the mix. As a coach, I've had lots of opportunities to practise, but it's become pretty routine to stay in discernment mode.

Discern

One thing I used to do is imagine myself speaking with a parent of any of the challenging people I've been tempted to judge, and I could always locate something lovable.

1. If I told Bobby Lee's mother that he seemed like a pretty lax fellow, some would say even lazy, she would sigh and murmur, "I know, but he's such a lovely boy. His mind wanders so! He loves his animals, up at all times feeding them and caring for them." *Hey,* I would exclaim to myself, *Bobby Lee's not lazy!*

2. If I told Lucy's mom that Lucy gets herself into terrible politics at the office, Lucy's mom would say, "Oh, that Lucy, she's always been getting herself into the mix of things. You should have seen her in high school. She just wants to be loved by her friends, is all. She was the youngest of her siblings, you know." *That's sweet,* I would think.

3. If I told Bartholomew's mother that he sure seemed arrogant and competitive and pushy, she would say, "Oh, and stubborn, too. Like that since he was a child. Wouldn't share his toys with anyone, no matter what you did. But he's a hard worker, that boy. You've got to love him for that." Seeing Bart as merely stubborn, assertive, and hard-working somehow takes the air out of my tires.

4. About Julia's tendency to be particularly crabby, her dad would say, "Oh, you don't want to get on her bad side. She'll eat you alive. That's what makes her special. She's protective, territorial, intensely competitive. A real high achiever, that one!" A parent's love does the trick.

The leader's challenge in handling employees is to see them as people despite the fact that, as grown-ups, they can get off track at work. These were somebody's kids once. Another perspective that keeps me on the safe side of the judgment fence with folks is the realization that most behaviour can be seen as two sides of the same coin. It has an upside and a downside.

About our four friends above:

1. Bobby Lee isn't lazy, per se. He's an introvert who isn't that into his current job. But the other side of that quiet presence is depth and a capacity to pour himself into what he loves.

2. Lucy, the political creature, might show her share of behind-the-scenes politicking, but the beautiful side of it is that she has a genuine craving to be at the heart of things.

3. Bartholomew might be quite pushy and dominating, but he's a natural at taking charge. The other side of his coin is the intensity of his will.

4. Julia might eat us alive, but that's balanced by her pure, protective nature.

My point here is that cultivating a culture that inspires people to step up to the plate requires you to ensure your perspective on people is free of judgment, or the trappings of judgment, and focuses on their lovability. This isn't to say that a leader needs to avoid emotion. Positive emotion, for example, can move mountains. And frustration is built right into the nature of commercialism, a primary driver of which is the condition of wanting more than we currently have. The key for the leader is in processing and expressing it. Perspective, the higher vantage point, a longer time horizon, the macro view, discerning level-headedness — these are what we want from leaders. They elevate us.

> Cultivating a culture that inspires people to step up to the plate requires you to ensure your perspective on people is free of judgment and focuses on their lovability.

SCULPTING YOUR CULTURE

Indeed, leaders need to

- make people feel heard, safe, and "bigger";
- connect with what people crave and help them deal with or even avoid what they fear;
- talk about what accountability, responsibility, and commitment look like and be the prototype for people to model;
- consistently nurture growth person by person;
- discern but not judge;
- elevate people's attention to a place above where they are now so they see what they're doing in a larger context;
- overtly, explicitly nurture autonomy; and
- create a convivial work environment.

As for what personal leadership *style* is most suitable for the target culture, that's no doubt up to each of us. Here is my own, in case it brings you value: *Be a warm, friendly, open, goal-oriented, nitpicky SOB.*

- By warm, I mean compassionate, humane, and sincere. This isn't about feigned warmth; it requires locating genuine compassion for another's being (it's in there!).
- By friendly, I mean creating an enjoyable environment. We have referred to it in this book as convivial and light. I would add nonconfrontational, particularly if you can embrace the notion that we're all wrestling with polarities in one way or another. As I said previously, it's not an "I'm right and you're wrong" context we seek but a "We're both right" one.
- By open, I mean inclined toward full disclosure, with discretion and political prudence in mind. Minimize secrecy. If you take the validating, we-are-all-wrestling-with-polarities orientation, then you can probably afford to be more open than you think. You can't tell secrets, and you shouldn't express your disappointments about other people with those below you, but you can talk about your noble motives and even your own failings. The odds are that if you're disappointed with the person sitting in front of you, then you could first consider how you've heretofore failed to steer him or her correctly. Own it first, before you even dream of blame.
- By goal-oriented, I mean always keeping an eye on the purpose, strategy, and objectives in the near term, mid-term, and long term in relation to yourself, your team, your team members, and your organization. The "arrow" of this will indeed be a fat one, but it should also be straight (such that all of those are heading in the same direction).
- By nitpicky, I mean glad, if not eager, to find the smallest details to measure someone's full participation in executing the standards and values of the organization. Go ahead. Everything matters. We're on a quest for perfection, after all. We might never reach it, and we might only be halfway so far, but we're on a mission.
- By SOB, I mean someone who will relentlessly pursue details until things are just plain precise, true, and up to snuff. Creating a humanistic environment doesn't preclude relentlessness; it just depends on how you express it in yourself and to others.

9
ORGANIZATIONAL ACCOUNTABILITY

This book has promoted a people-centric or *humanistic* environment. The word *compassion* has come up at least a dozen times. We have talked about ideas like self-acceptance, being non-judgmental, and forgiveness; the words *feel* and *feelings* have been used over 250 times. Generally, we've been discussing a softer side of life at work. These things don't sound like accountability; at least, not in the sense of "holding people to account."

When most of us think about accountability, we think of some kind of confrontation potentially resulting in consequences, as in the declaration, "We must hold someone accountable for this mess," or "Who's to blame for this?" or "Someone has to pay!" The buck, after all, must stop somewhere.

Actually, for simplicity, I differentiate between two types of accountability: outside and inside. Outside accountability concerns a person or organization being accountable to an entity such as the justice system, a regulatory entity, shareholders, the media, and thereby the electorate — an authority outside the organization. Inside accountability pertains to people being accountable to other people within their organization. The key distinction between the two is who is holding whom accountable.

They do share certain traits, of course. In both cases, the people who tend to behave responsibly more often succeed in their roles, people know they might have to account for themselves, and extenuating circumstances are quite relevant to determinations of culpability and consequences. But there are differences beyond who is holding whom accountable. Outside accountability operates at a societal level. It has more official overtones and, in the absence of extenuating circumstances, usually involves big, serious consequences imposed by the outside party. It typically relies on relatively strict laws, rules, requirements, and regulations.

Often senior leaders want the trappings of outside accountability for their organization because of its weightiness and the clarity they perceive it possesses, but the tangible consequences associated with the gravity of formally stipulated positions bring several disadvantages. Outside accountability tends to create a by-the-book culture that, for example, makes customers feel as if they're interacting with a bureaucracy rather than with people. Inside accountability, being more about people than the presumably purely objective assessment driven by, for example, the "long arm of the law," has an extra layer of muddiness to it because people import their own subjectivity and variability to the accountability. For instance, the rules or standards of inside organizations are often unclear, even if they're written, and there are often multiple judges to apply those standards, such as my boss, my former boss, my boss's boss, and my dotted-line boss.

> In the culture we've been talking about in this book, autonomy and individuality are celebrated and people are self-accountable — they use their organization to achieve their own goals, and their employer reaps the benefits.

But in the right culture, modelled by the right leaders, inside accountability can yield the performance and results that even the fussiest of senior leaders can't argue with. That's one point of this book. Inside accountability can be profound if it's managed properly. Of the hundreds of companies I've worked with intimately, those with what we've been referring to as a "culture of genuine accountability" tend to be the more productive, profitable, creative, and successful competitors. And they happen to enjoy lower employee turnover and generally happier employees. The lesser organizations either lament the lack of accountability or have militaristic accountability. They have heretofore failed to navigate their way between the two.

In the culture we've been talking about in this book, autonomy and individuality are celebrated and people are self-accountable (that is, they're responsible to themselves in addition to the organization, and they're what you would call responsible people). They're committed and they execute. They don't blame and they don't fall into a defensive mode. They're using their organization to achieve their own goals, and their employer reaps the benefits. They grow in their learning culture and they tend toward loyalty.

The leaders of such organizations whom I most respect seem to project a certain style that promotes all of these things. It's a style that adopts the dictum from the last chapter: warm, friendly, open, but also goal-oriented, persistent, and — to put the last term (*SOB*) from the previous chapter into perspective — totally comfortable with sitting in silence while the person across from them struggles to collect his or her thoughts to answer calm but direct questions often punctuated by pregnant gaps. There can be compassion in those moments — I would say there should be — but there's also a fulsome, existential hunger to know: "Help me understand why you chose to do it this way." Indeed, the approach from a highly and personally responsible, self-esteem-supporting leader not interested in blame but totally inclined toward creating a culture of neither hardball nor softball, but what I like to call realball, is powerful and appealing and has a provocative imminence about it.

REALBALL

Unlike realball, hardball is the stuff of tough conversations in which coercive influence techniques are brought to bear — raised voices, finger pointing, and sounds of anger. It's fear-producing and defence-goading. Softball is the opposite. It's about letting people off the hook — being a softie who approaches accountability reluctantly and maybe fearfully. With this approach, leaders ask about things but don't address bad faith. This is the style I see most often because, for most of us, holding people accountable feels like work; consequences are introduced only after things have deteriorated. Softball style in inside accountability is probably the natural state for companies unless somebody makes a mission out of improving accountability.

The impulses that drive modern leaders to seek greater stringencies are the same impulses that led to the emergence of social accountability in the first place. People need policing. The problem is that getting too aggressive is inelegant.

And then there's realball. This is the style being espoused in this book. Realball requires leaders to be discerning but not allow themselves to leap to personal value judgments upon hearing an answer to a question. It requires a genuinely empathetic sense of "Okay, I can see where you're coming from on that" (that is, to actually see where the person is coming from). And then it calls for action planning because, of course, we're in this to achieve our targets and we're committed. The implicit messaging, maybe even explicit, is: "I respect you, I honour you, I see you. And what's done is done." Then, after the action plan has been explicitly stated (so there's no hazy accountability), such a leader would say, powerfully and even caringly, "At this moment we're committed, yes?" And then, "And I'm committed to you and to making this work." Pregnant, pregnant moment, then, "Where are you on all this?" And after a reply, "May I ask you why?"

> A leader engaged in realball is interested in truth, commitment, personal responsibility, self-responsibility, and, tangibly speaking, people living by their word.

The possible next steps in such a conversation abound. What they all have in common is a fearless, patient, goal-oriented quest to get real. A leader engaged in realball is interested in truth, commitment, personal responsibility, self-responsibility, and, tangibly speaking, people living by their word.

We said above that there was an imminence built into the style. By that we mean the self-responsible leader brings his full attention to conversational moments. He collects his thoughts and musters his will to address a subject. He's on the lookout for what's true and calls out confusion when he hears it or feels it within himself. Out of his own integrity, he has "skin in the game." He owes it to himself to be genuine, to not let himself off the hook for getting to the bottom of things, and for holding on to his responsibility to others to be respectful and caring — thus, he allows for pauses to let the other person find his own truth. Those quiet moments are often where real accountability comes from. They're attention-rousing and sincere; inviting and safe; truth-focused, powerful, and productive.

In an *outside* accountability circumstance, a lawyer, in front of a court judge, might ask, "Why did you do that?" and the person being held accountable can't help but run in the back of her mind an algorithm that weighs the consequences and viability of each possible response. But in an *inside* accountability circumstance, when a self-responsible leader, one responsible for the whole panoply of traits we've been discussing in this book — caring but goal-oriented — poses the question, the person being held accountable, knowing that this boss's style will be here tomorrow and in the foreseeable future, is much more likely to reflect sincerely and find the truth.

So that we can all get on with it, let's muster from our hearts a new commitment, bring our full attention to it during these profound moments, align our words with our intentions, and throw our stuff off the proverbial plane — *oommmph!*

So how does one institutionalize such a realball approach in a culture of inside accountability? That's the question we now need to look at. And we'll do so, of course, on the assumption that in such an environment, productivity, morale, and overall results are superior. The leader is happier, the employee is happier, the organization is productive, and everybody grows.

SIGNS AND SYMPTOMS

Just to build your fluency with the distinctions we've been making about the two types of accountability and the styles of leadership pertaining to accountability, let's look at an example that reveals a readiness for some kind of accountability intervention. The story, which doesn't end particularly well, at least from my limited point of view, will reveal my own simple thinking process when I hear about accountability issues.

A friend of mine works in the New York office of an international conglomerate (not a client). He says to me that his workplace has a serious accountability problem. "Nobody does what they're supposed to do," and "Nobody holds people accountable for the fact that they don't, so everybody gets away with everything and mistakes are made all over the place."

As you would expect from someone writing about the need to avoid generalizations and premature judgments, I detect the sweeping characterizations and try to hold my active hypotheses somewhat tentatively. One hypothesis is that my friend is quite emotionally engaged by the matter, and there's probably somebody in the local chain of command who is, for some reason, not calling people to task. I decide to conversationally work my way down from the top. I pose the next question: "What does the guy in charge of the New York office think about the problem?"

"He can't stand it, but he doesn't do anything about it."

Instantly, I think to myself, *Got it. The local leader is a softie. Needs to learn realball instead of softball. Time to check whether it starts with him or flows through him from an even higher place in the hierarchy.*

"And what does his boss think about it?" I ask.

"He operates out of Paris," my friend says. "He hates it. He complains that the New York guy has an accountability problem. He's geographically too far away to spend enough time in the New York office, but from what I hear, depending on what happens when our numbers come out a few months from now, heads will roll."

Ah, the New York guy hasn't got control and feels badly about it. Results are probably not so good (but I'm not sure whose results we're talking about here). The Paris guy smells that things are out of control and wants to play hardball (he wants the trappings of outside accountability). I'm thinking that Paris would be happy with some kind of intervention in New York to get things under control, depending on whether the New York boss could politically afford to own that there was a problem to be solved. Even though folks in his office would attest to his hating the problem, would he defend himself up the ladder, or would he take ownership, or would his boss be enlightened enough to avoid blame and just jump on the opportunity to fix the problem?

I feel as if I could establish a relationship with the New York–based leader. I could help him discover the obstacles holding him back from changing the culture. Perhaps he's a fearful fellow, or overloaded with problems, or experiencing a dissonance between valuing people who live by their word and his own reluctance to call them on it when they don't.

The New York leader and I get on the phone for a call set up by my acquaintance. Right off the bat, I interpret his readiness to have a conversation as a sign that he's likely open to help. I discover that this is a man wrestling with a very diverse array of issues, and though he recognizes that accountability is one of them, it's not very high on his list. He cites that two of the people who report directly to him are "extremely assertive" and are "not likely to be tamed." And despite the blame orientation of their two cultures, their results are strong. They pay no apparent attention to unfulfilled promises. And he hypothesizes that they're both connected to senior Paris people who respect them for being so influential.

From the point of view of a consultant unpacking a team dynamic, the situation wasn't really unusual. There was a softball style on the part of the senior New York player; he quickly admitted he was fearful and highly judgmental of the self-absorbed style of the two assertive people who report to him. He also acknowledged that for the entire New York senior team, the accountabilities were hazy at best. There were no job descriptions and no agreed-upon values.

There was a clear opportunity for an intervention. I could see it. Paris would sign off because that leader knew there was a problem. The New York leader would be relieved because he could potentially change the culture despite the two tough cookies. *Who knows?* he might think. *Maybe their hardball could be converted to realball.* After all, the intensity of realball can be alluring to traditional hardballers. And the New York leader himself would be eager to shift from softball to realball. That possibility is also usually alluring to softies because it doesn't call for aggression — just integrity. This, as far as I was concerned, was quite workable.

However, things often don't unfold as we would like or predict. Within two weeks, the New York man's employment was terminated by the Paris-based leader. One of the two powerhouse deputies referred to above was promoted to run the New York office, and within another month, he terminated a variety of mid-level leaders, some of whom, according to my friend, were the "problem people." I moved on.

What would a project such as this have looked like? It would depend on the scope of the mission. As we're about to discuss, a network-wide initiative (for example, the New York regional office with multiple departments) would be much more complex than a single department. Either way the basics of accountability are prerequisites. Let's look.

INSTITUTIONALIZING ACCOUNTABILITY

In this book, I've referred to the basic, systemic elements of organizational accountability. That is, even *before* an intervention to engender personal responsibility, there are certain steps leaders are smart to take to create a context for accountability. It's rare for an organization *not* to have most of the following in place, but they are all advantageous for both outside and inside accountability systems. Leaders must

1. define the whole organization's mission (as in, why do we exist as an entity?) and socialize it;
2. create a vision of where they want to take their organization;
3. establish what values or operating principles they want to live by;
4. create a strategy to fulfill their vision;
5. set objectives for what they want to accomplish and by when;
6. establish milestones along the way toward their objectives so they can assess and see progress;
7. create clear job descriptions so that each contributor knows his or her role;
8. define the skills and knowledge required by people in order to meet the objectives;
9. hire people based on the target skills and knowledge;
10. set personalized objectives for each contributor;
11. track each contributor against those objectives;
12. regularly touch base with each contributor concerning gaps between objectives and performance;
13. educate contributors regarding how they can optimize performance;
14. compensate contributors for successful performance;
15. establish milestones for "recovering" (fixing) contributors who have failed to produce; and
16. make it clear to contributors what will happen if objectives are repeatedly not fulfilled.

With some version of each of these in place, an organization, big or small, is ready for the kind of cultural adjustment implied by elevating the sense of personal responsibility shared by each member of the community. That is, we're about to discuss how to create a culture of genuine accountability — inside accountability with a healthy dose of realball.

Of course, a small team of five players and a huge organization of thousands are both organizations, but the latter needs a somewhat more detailed, complex plan to create the target environment. So let's treat them differently, starting with advice to the leader who is focused mostly on her small team. Then we'll unpack the larger mission.

A PARTY OF FIVE

Let's say you lead a team of five people and you want to shift its culture toward greater accountability — trying to get people to step up to the plate more independently, be less likely to blame and self-defend, and generally move in a more focused fashion toward the team's goal. Productivity is the name of the game, of course, but so, too, is job satisfaction — not just for you but for everybody.

Put Your Finger on the Desired Change

To take advantage of the sequence of steps below, whether it's to execute something in this book or to make any kind of small team-culture change, it's smart to label what you're trying to accomplish even before you start talking about it with others. Below is a list of 12 distinct directions, any or all of which would be worthy of team pursuit. They would all contribute to the culture of accountability we've been discussing.

1. Be more personally responsible to others and ourselves.
2. Take more ownership (in other words, blame less).
3. Fully commit to objectives or to values.
4. Stay focused (avoid distractions).
5. Sustain a positive attitude.
6. Engage in full-disclosure communication.
7. Improve self-talk.
8. Be fearless on the job.
9. Break through bad faith.
10. Be discerning rather than judgmental.
11. Actively build a learning culture.
12. Support each other (in other words, self-esteem for all!).

Each of the above items might appear to be intangible and difficult to make a mission out of, but each of them can be explored in this book and be further unpacked in a team discussion. When you raise them in conversation after a bit of discussion and perhaps some examples, people will know what you're talking about.

Express Your Desire

Assemble the troops and tell them your thoughts. Reveal how you know how people feel these days (whatever that is — the idea is to connect with what is likely running through their minds). Describe what you want the culture of the team to look like. Try to be specific about what you would like to see and hear (for example, laughter in the halls, people saying "I own it," people expressing positive things about others, making explicit commitments, more note-taking, a dollar in the jar every time we say bad things about other departments). After showing your group that you identify with its perspective these days and clarifying your vision for the group, proceed with the following agenda steps for your meeting:

1. Explain how your vision would make things better for everyone and for the organization. Read portions of this book out loud, if that suits you.
2. Say that you're committed and willing to be held responsible by any of them each time you breach your word.
3. Talk about the learning culture and how it means humbly giving each other feedback so that they can learn. Discuss how harmful blame and defensiveness can be.
4. Encourage lots of discussion so that everyone is clear on, contributes to, and buys in to the vision.
5. Consider naming the initiative so that people can refer to it over time. Create a legacy for the group.

Clearly Set the Standards

We said that you shouldn't be judgmental, but that doesn't mean you can't be discerning — and discerning means seeing differences between how things ought to be versus how they are, while keeping your big-picture perspective. So, perhaps in the meeting outlined in the previous section, or in subsequent conversations, work with your group to set standards — perhaps ways we want to work together, reduced error rates, improved communication styles, team values to which all genuinely subscribe, your style as a leader, frequency of meetings, performance conversations, routine topics for performance conversations, or team and individual objectives. The point is that we need objectives to aspire to, including performance goals, as well as activities and routines to achieve those goals beyond what we have now.

Have One-on-One Dialogues

On at least a monthly basis, but possibly even on a weekly basis, you should be meeting, preferably face to face, with your team members to specifically discuss how they're doing against their broad targets. Regular meetings might already be a given for you or already entrenched in your organization's performance management system, but it's during these meetings that you practise your enlightened leadership skills: support self-esteem, be discerning but not judgmental, and punctuate discussions with realball thinking (for instance, don't let things go). The biggest opportunity during one-on-one meetings is to facilitate learning. In fact, make it a goal that each time you meet, the person walks away with insight as well as with a sense of feeling bigger instead of being diminished in spirit.

> It's during one-on-one meetings that you practise your enlightened leadership skills: support self-esteem, be discerning but not judgmental, and punctuate discussions with realball thinking.

For most leaders, being supportive, non-judgmental, and inclined to solicit and make sincere, if not intense, commitments is easiest when things are rosy. But it's when objectives or promises haven't been met that supportive realball leadership is put to the test. In such challenging times, remember to slow the conversation down with pauses and open questions (rather than yes-or-no questions) such as "Why?" Don't hesitate to get real and disclose, even if the moment is awkward.

Below is a list of sentences that some existential, realball, highly authentic, supportive, but only-interested-in-the-truth leaders have been heard to utter. I offer them not as a script but just to give you a flavour for what accountability can look like, particularly during tough times, when executed in the way we've been describing. In each case, there's a problem, and the sentences and questions are meant to go into the problem, to crack it open, if you will, to let some light in.

1.   What do you think I should do about *that*?
2.   We can't pretend that's okay in the future. What will you do differently? What will be different? How can I help?
3.   I totally want to support you and I totally don't want this to get messed up. This is a deal breaker for me (as in, I don't know what I'll do, but it's hot). So we need to unpack it more. Tell me much more about …
4.   I'm not really comfortable with how things are going. How are you with it all?
5.   Here are my concerns … As this list stands, things aren't working for me. We need to see a transformation, and I aim to help make it happen.
6.   I don't think what you just said is going to be enough for where we need to take this thing. I need more from you. Let's take this apart.
7.   You say *xyz*, and I hear you, but I don't really see any change at all. Help me understand what's happening. Why am I not seeing results?
8.   What do you want me to do if this happens again? I'm not trying to be funny here. Honestly, what should I do?
9.   Do you want to know what I think? Correct me where I'm wrong, but I think you …
10. I find myself having to manage my frustration about this. I own the frustration — I mean, it's mine to address. I do want to tell you about it. It feels to me like …
11. Let's turn up the volume a bit on staying focused. Why don't you and I touch base every few [hours, days] so we can stay close. We've established that you want to do better and that things take you away. Let me be your support vehicle. Let's connect … a lot. You can lean on me.

Each of the heavier dialogues listed above needs to end with something positive, hopeful, sincere, and warm. Having existential showdowns loaded with relatively intense robust moments isn't supposed to be punishment; instead, it's about getting at the truth, and the truth is almost always good. I would venture to suggest that being a good leader is about inspiring, even though sometimes mid-dialogue, for example, it's personally awkward for the other person.

Set and Follow Personal Rules

It's smart for you to make a list of 10 to 40 rules that you'll live by at least at work. Pull some of them right from this book if you want. But also add some routines such as cleaning your work station at the end of every day; booking meetings with employees in advance, even before you know what you want to talk about; sending out positive notes to the team or to individuals on a regular basis; and posting your near-term and mid-term objectives somewhere very visible and changing the location every day so you don't ignore the posting.

Ensure your rules fulfill your ambition to create a learning culture. For example, make a list of each person on your team and figure out individual learning opportunities. Ask yourself what you're going to do to help the person. Diarize it. Also, as indicated above, make sure the learning topic is brought up during most of your one-on-one meetings. A template is available at www.horn.com/insights that you can download and complete for this purpose.

Close the Loop

A closed-loop system, of course, is one in which there are no loose ends flailing about that can make things unravel. And, as discussed in Chapter 3, your best intentions, particularly when they're about team-culture matters, need some tools brought to bear to keep them alive. There are several little things you can do to make this initiative stick:

1. Create an image in your mind that reflects why you want to do this. Feel that image in your bones and bring that image to mind regularly (such as at the start of meetings).
2. Announce your commitments to your team members (so you'll be more likely to stick to them).
3. Tell your boss you've undertaken a team-culture initiative.
4. Invite those who report to you directly to hold you accountable to your commitments concerning this initiative.
5. Book group meetings in advance so that people's schedules remind you and everyone that you're on a mission together.
6. Consider amending bonus plans so that they address elements of the initiative. For example, if error rates go down, people earn more.

The key point about making department-wide culture changes is to visualize them, label them, define them behaviourally, socialize them, track or measure them, and revisit them regularly.

LARGE ORGANIZATIONS

Now it's time to visualize how to institutionalize a culture of genuine accountability in a large organization. To see it in its most practical form, we're talking about a *learning initiative* — a series of communications and learning events that move people farther on a desirable, unending path. It's a cultural path that, once started, lives in an organization for years, and all employees carry elements of what they learned for the rest of their careers. I still have people reach out to me years after they were exposed to some of the ideas we've discussed in this book and report how they "took it home," meaning that not only did it help them on the job, but in their private life, as well. That's because finding personal responsibility and self-responsibility, and being a part of a culture of continuous improvement, has enduring influence on a person's life. Genuine accountability becomes a personal thing, even when top management changes. Children are affected, after all, when a parent discovers the wisdom and personal power that emanates from assuming personal responsibility.

Execution

The items that follow are a compilation of everything in this book that can be institutionalized. It assumes the reader already has the basics installed — items such as those listed as prerequisites above — and wants to create a culture of *genuine* accountability, one in which people may be held to account, but also one in which they're willing to *hold themselves* to account. That, after all, is what makes it genuine.

> A culture of *genuine* accountability is not just one in which people may be held to account, but also one in which they're willing to *hold themselves* to account.

To be clear, such a venture is this book's answer to the lament of senior leaders who sense there isn't enough accountability in their organization. We're saying here that, rather than getting stricter in the way that outside accountability imposes tests and consequences, we're smart to work from the inside and create an environment where people *want* to be more responsible.

That calls for an intervention that educates people at all levels about personal responsibility. The most efficient means to provide this education is to focus on the leadership group; they're the people who can instill the values and behaviours of full personal responsibility for all.

The items below start with visualizing a campaign to accomplish the task. In that sense, they're somewhat in chronological order.

Create a Budget

There's a cost to such a venture, both in terms of money and time, but the hard costs inherent in an accountability initiative can be less than one might think. If an organization chooses, for example, to pull from a book like this one the main thoughts and assigns internal designers to create learning events that behaviouralize the main points, there are no increases in overhead other than potential travel costs to bring people together and marketing costs to promote the initiative, all of which can be minimal.

Going externally for support on the initiative is another option. Having been engaged to provide such support, my experience is that a community of 5,000 employees could spend between $1.5 and $2.5 million over four years, assuming a pyramid-shaped organizational structure with a ratio of eight front-line employees per front-line leader; labour costs don't rise when time is spent in learning situations; and no travel costs are involved. Over that period, each leader would require a total of seven days of learning, and front-line employees would each be exposed to two days of learning (above whatever skills training they receive normally). Efficiencies in execution improve, of course, if the size of the community is greater, since marketing and facilitator enablement costs are distributed across more learners. In this case, the cost per employee would go down.

Another cost to be considered is the actual time required of leaders to build the culture being discussed in this book. Although to a certain extent it's the nature of conversations they have with those who report directly to them that will make the difference (such that no additional "management time" is required), there also might be an increase in the number of conversations they need to participate in. For example, if leaders are committed to more coaching sessions per employee per unit of time, then at least in the short term there might be less of their time available for administrative work. This can drive up costs, but not a lot.

Plan to Measure Results

It's difficult to measure results, of course, because we never know whether the main contributors to improvements to volume, profit, share, profitability, or employee retention and satisfaction levels can be traced to cultural changes. However, those are the key metrics to monitor. Keeping in mind that leadership skills are the key point of leverage in this kind of initiative, it makes sense for leaders to do pre- and post-measurements on the extent to which those who report directly to them feel that, for example, they're valued by them.

My experience with many initiatives of this nature is that anecdotal results are as convincing to everyone — stakeholders and outsiders — as any effort to quantify proofs of return on investment. There's nothing more pleasurable than having a chief operating officer of a five billion dollar company say to you at dinner, before any wine has been served, "You know, this really has worked. I can see it in the way our people think and operate, and I can see it in the way we talk to customers. I can't prove it mathematically, but I can see it with my own two eyes." Such a remark can bring the leader of a learning company that has poured its soul into a venture such as this to tears.

Gain Executive Sponsorship

It's obviously very important that executives not only approve of the initiative but embody the values embedded in it, as well. If mid-level leaders are going to learn how to coach people, contribute support, and conduct probing conversations, for instance, then senior leaders need to learn it, too. The probability of success directly correlates with the involvement of senior players. I've seen senior leaders (in organizations exceeding 50,000 employees) actually learn to deliver training, let alone to kick off all training sessions.

Brand the Initiative

Although I wouldn't use the word *accountability* in the title of your initiative, I do know that a name and logo help hugely. People need to see the project as a permanent shift in culture derived from values, mission, and strategy. Companies are smart to "thingize" the style of operating being espoused. I have often seen organizations adopt the key learning from this book (for example, the principles of self-esteem support, taking personal responsibility, and managing self-talk) and translate it into target outcomes, thereby not speaking at all about intangibles or more provocative notions such as accountability. For example, an organization that seeks to put the customer first needs to teach leaders all of the exact same principles. Customer-centricity, after all, is perhaps one result of getting people to take responsibility for doing the right thing.

Market the Brand

Initiatives such as this require a rigorous communications strategy that involves multiple hits, continued use of the logo, and follow-up communications around all learning events. Boardroom walls can be decked with posters pointing to and describing things like "What we believe in"; "How we talk around here"; and "Touch it, own it." We said earlier that individuals will retain some of these ideas as gifts, but from the point of view of the broader organizational culture, the passage of time, a change in leadership, and normal employee turnover rates can diminish the ideological impact. I know of several organizations that have kept the culture-change initiative alive by means of a sustained, dynamic marketing plan.

Immerse Executives First

Cascading from top to bottom is the way to go. Executive sessions can be compressed, but not too much. Although it's true for all groups being exposed to the ideas inherent in the accountability culture, the credibility of the facilitator conducting sessions is critical.

Plan System-Wide Education

Senior leaders, front-line people, and everyone in between need to be exposed to certain consistent messaging (for example, "We support self-esteem"; "How to keep your own commitments"; "Where willpower comes from"), but only leaders need to learn how to conduct conversations focused on the principles in this book (such as holding people accountable). Front-line employees should be told what to expect — for example, your boss is going to ask challenging questions, but you'll be supported unconditionally as you're encouraged to address the obstacles that hold you back from achieving your goals.

Consider What Satellite Systems Need to Change

It's important that there's alignment between the systems that people work with on a daily basis and the values they're learning to adopt in their daily work. For example, if salespeople are charged up with their reasonably aggressive goals, and they've mustered the personal commitment but are burdened by an order system that can't keep pace, then the misalignment will cause a backfire. Or if leaders, upon realizing they'll have to spend more time with their people, are suddenly sent on a mission that consumes the time they planned to create the target culture, then they'll roll their eyes and things will fall apart.

Integrate into Current Performance Management

Most companies have a system to track employee performance and meet with employees to discuss performance against key performance indicators. This system should be rewired to incorporate the values, behaviours, and activities implied by infusing genuine, warm accountability. For example, the system should be revamped to accommodate the answers to questions such as, "How often should our leaders meet with those who report directly to them?" and, "How will we measure employee satisfaction and hold our leaders accountable for improving?"

Create a Learning Strategy

A master plan for educating people concerning this initiative is called for, addressing things like the *how* (classroom, webinars, asynchronous e-learning tools, virtual classrooms, mobile apps, chat bots), a learning map by audience type, and a rollout plan that addresses geography and links to normally scheduled meetings. The strategy should also address who will design and deliver training, and over what period training by a third-party provider will be required, if at all. To what extent is the organization able to deliver on the initiative independently?

Educate

Content for such an initiative can come from sources such as this book. Employees at all levels can learn the answers to questions such as, "How do I ... ?"

- hold myself responsible
- respond to blame
- handle misfortune and mistakes
- decide to apologize, and how do I then apologize
- exhibit more responsibility just as a person on the planet
- feel about my job, and how committed am I
- connect my obligations to what I crave in my life
- locate my bad faith and break through it
- close my eyes and leap to commitment
- do what I say I will do
- create commitment devices for myself
- weave new behaviours into my life
- build my own self-esteem
- ask for help
- overcome my fears
- manage my self-talk
- improve my work–life balance
- manage my boss

Leaders will want to know the answers to questions such as, "How do I … ?"

- be a better listener
- make people feel understood
- confront people without judging them
- stay in discernment mode
- have a conversation that manifests the values of self-esteem support, goal-orientation, and authenticity
- deal with someone who doesn't do what was promised
- help someone to discover obstacles to personal responsibility
- inspire a sense of team
- coach someone to improve performance
- coach someone to become more responsible
- delegate autonomy
- resist my temptation to control
- locate the extent to which I buy into my mission and to which I'm effective at getting my team to buy into it
- create and contribute to a learning culture

WRAP-UP

I've heard that with respect to responsibility, there are three or four phases in our lives: first we're dependent (as kids, when others are responsible for us); then we become independent (as teenagers, when we gradually become more responsible for ourselves); then, if we land with a partner, we're codependent (such that, relying on each other, the partners are readied to increase their responsibility load, and perhaps even find themselves nurturing each other); and finally we're interdependent (as fully grown adults recognizing we're responsible for the whole kit and caboodle — ourselves, our loved ones, the things we touch, and perhaps the world). So I suspect we're in this together: evolving as self-responsible agents while we take on more responsibility for the world in which we operate and live. I don't think either evolution ever stops.

Often the transitions are prolonged and clumsy at best. My own transition from dependence to independence, for example, involved a fair bit of self-absorption that steered me toward meditation, psychotherapy, and the study of psychology and philosophy. All of this facilitated the emergence of independence and early hints of responsibility in the world. I'm pretty sure I started in my career in this space — with the secret that I was mostly interested in myself. I could talk about being responsible, and portray being responsible, but I can see now that at the time I was still partially blocked by my self-absorption. Codependency made me feel

> We're in this together: evolving as self-responsible agents while we take on more responsibility for the world in which we operate and live.

much more secure in my existence, and somewhere in that security emerged a genuine interest in the conscious experiences of others. I could emotionally afford to help them carry their load, and I had enough of my own uneasy history to bring some value because, in my own way, I had been there.

Now open space has become a part of my being. I find myself genuinely interested in others and am predisposed to wonder about whoever is in front of me professionally: What's it like to be you? Are you okay in your quest to get what you deeply crave in your life? If you could stretch yourself just a bit more — as long as you want to, of course — how would you behave differently? What do you think is holding you back from doing this? If you could accomplish whatever it is that you truly want, what would you do to make that happen?

I suppose a few decades of a gradually emerging interdependence sensibility, and the recognition that stepping up to the plate is sort of the name of the game, has led to this book and to its main formula: *getting people to become more responsible is the essence of solving day-to-day accountability problems.* If I had another lifetime and could take a different career direction, I would seek to quantify the utility of the 10 precepts below that summarize this book.

> Getting people to become more responsible is the essence of solving day-to-day accountability problems.

1. Nurture genuine accountability by valuing personal responsibility — promote doing the responsible thing.
2. Play realball, not hardball or softball. Create ripe moments.
3. Ensure people actually believe what they're promising.
4. Do what you say and own your mistakes.
5. Elevate people: educate, communicate the bigger picture, and act as a model for doing the responsible thing.
6. Tap into what people want in their hearts, and align their job descriptions and assignments accordingly.
7. Discern and act when appropriate; do not judge.
8. Ignore blame and defence; focus on the array of contributing factors in problems, and on planning and execution.
9. Know your people. Make them feel heard, safe, and valued. All the time.
10. Promote perspective. That's where the light is brightest.

If you aren't a leader of others, at least by profession, then you have responsibility to, and for, surely one of the most important people in the world. Here's that same list reframed accordingly:

1. Allow yourself to listen to your own thoughts about doing the responsible thing. Discern whether those thoughts come from a place you can trust, then choose consciously.
2. In your interactions with others, neither a toughie nor a softie be. Stand up for yourself, and seek and present the truth as much as you can.

3. Bring your awareness to bear when you promise. Treat living by your word as a moral responsibility in addition to a responsibility you have to yourself.

4. Own your mistakes, then self-forgive.

5. Be seen doing the responsible thing. And do it in private, too.

6. Consciously connect what you must do with what you want to do. For example, there is a reason you're doing it.

7. Discern and then act when appropriate; resist being judgmental.

8. Ignore blame and defence; focus on the array of contributing factors in problems and move toward solutions.

9. Take time for yourself every single day. Get as acquainted as possible with your quiet time; compared to all the things you do, it's the closest one to you.

10. Find ways to regain your perspective on life and shine that light on your day-to-day.

All things in this book considered, accountability starts with the dialogue you have with yourself. If you're a leader of many, you're the one who must manage your impulses to be anything other than in full connection with the people you lead: supportive, committed, skilled at walking that fine line between discerning and judging, and consistently reaching to take more responsibility. It's work.

Regarding you personally, whether a leader of others or not, you're responsible for your body, your reactions, your satisfaction, and fulfilling your commitments not just to others but also to yourself. This takes the ability to regularly rise above yourself and your daily vicissitudes to regain your wiser perspective. That place is the source of your willpower, your wisdom, and your integrity. From that place you hold yourself accountable, because you can and you're worthy of the mission.

ACKNOWLEDGEMENTS

Of course, none of my friends and loved ones were actually accountable for helping me with this book; they did it out of the goodness of their hearts and maybe to help me avoid embarrassing myself. Assisting me by reading each chapter and being open, direct, and profoundly valuable in their feedback were my wife, Joan Berman; my daughter, Melissa Horn; and my colleague Lisa Tomassetti.

Other colleagues — Lynne Gallacher, Sean Verhoeven, and Lisa Young — made sure I was true to what we stand for at our company, HORN, and they nourished my thinking. Still more people from HORN subjected themselves to my requests for aid and came through swimmingly: Adrienne Camilleri, Alan Roth, Ashley Sprogis, Barry Kirkey, Deena Kruzic, Graham Kaufmann, Jeff Geady, Lindsay Valve, Steve Dennis, and Tim Dougan each played very specific roles in the production of the material, ranging from cover design to assessment refinement to general ideology. They also answered grey area questions, such as, "Hey, is this too wacky?" "Is this too personal?" "Is this an accurate statement?"

There is no doubt every client that I or my company has served over the past 30 years, the thousands of learning participants who have allowed us into their professional and even personal lives, and everyone I've ever coached has contributed to my best understanding of the topics inside this book. And since I continue to learn something new from every conversation with the people who explore their circumstances with me, this gratitude is directed as much to future clients I'll have the pleasure to serve as it is to past and present clients.

Last but not least, since in many respects he's the one who made it happen, I owe a debt of gratitude to my editor, Michael Carroll, whose publishing industry knowledge and editing acumen have made the process of producing this book, with the hefty support of the folks at Dundurn, as smooth as it could be.

In closing, I should also mention that the names of the people mentioned in this book have all been changed, and even the circumstances attributed to them have been juggled, all to ensure absolute privacy. Any correlation to any one person or organization would be a coincidence.

NOTES

CHAPTER 4: WILLPOWER

1. M.J. Crockett, "Restricting Temptations: Neural Mechanisms of Precommitment," *Neuron* 79, no. 2 (July 2013): 391–401.
2. Daniel Kahneman, *Thinking, Fast and Slow* (New York: Farrar, Straus and Giroux, 2011).
3. Martin E.P. Seligman, *Learned Optimism: How to Change Your Mind and Your Life* (New York: Pocket Books, 1992).
4. Tobias Kalenscher, *Decisions in the Brain: The Role of the Avian Forebrain (Nidopallium Caudolaterale) in Decision-Making* (Sarrebrücken, Germany: VDM Verlag, 2008).
5. Vanessa M. Patrick and Henrik Hagtvedt, "I Don't Versus I Can't: When Empowered Refusal Motivates Goal-Directed Behavior," *Journal of Consumer Research* 39, no. 2 (2012): 371–81.
6. Roberto Assagioli, *The Act of Will* (New York: Penguin, 1974).
7. Piero Ferrucci, *What We May Be* (New York: J.P. Tarcher, 1982).
8. Ibid.
9. Daniel Siegel, *Mindsight: Change Your Brain and Your Life* (New York: Random House, 2010).
10. Assagioli, *The Act of Will.*
11. Siegel, *Mindsight.*
12. Nathaniel Branden, *The Psychology of Self-Esteem* (New York: Bantam, 1969).
13. Carl R. Rogers and Fritz J. Roethlisberger, "Barriers and Gateways

to Communication," *Harvard Business Review* (November/December 1991, reprint).

14. Megan Oaten and Ken Cheng, "Longitudinal Gains in Self-Regulation from Regular Physical Exercise," *British Journal of Health Psychology* 11, part 4 (November 2006): 717–33.

15. M. Scott Peck, *The Road Less Traveled and Beyond: Spiritual Growth in an Age of Anxiety* (New York: Simon & Schuster, 1997).

CHAPTER 5: FREE OF BLAME

1. Morris B. Hoffman, *The Punisher's Brain: The Evolution of Judge and Jury* (Cambridge, MA: Cambridge University Press, 2014).

2. James P. Carse, *Breakfast at the Victory: The Mysticism of Ordinary Experience* (Toronto: HarperCollins Canada, 1995).

3. Eric Berne, *Games People Play: The Psychology of Human Relationships* (New York: Penguin, 1973).

4. Karina Schumann, "An Affirmed Self and a Better Apology: The Effect of Self-Affirmation on Transgressors' Responses to Victims," *Journal of Experimental Social Psychology* 54 (September 2014): 89–96.

5. Mahatma Gandhi, *All Men Are Brothers: Autobiographical Reflections*, ed. Krishna Kripalani (Paris: UNESCO/Columbia University Press, 1958).

CHAPTER 6: THE TWELVE OBSTACLES

1. Rogers and Roethlisberger, "Barriers and Gateways to Communication."
2. Ibid.

CHAPTER 8: BEING THE BOSS

1. Seligman, *Learned Optimism*.
2. Rogers and Roethlisberger, "Barriers and Gateways to Communication."
3. Debbie Ford, *The Dark Side of the Light Chasers* (New York: Riverhead Books, 1998).

BIBLIOGRAPHY

Ariely, Dan. *The (Honest) Truth About Dishonesty*. New York: HarperCollins, 2012.

Assagioli, Roberto. *The Act of Will*. New York: Penguin, 1974.

Berne, Eric. *Games People Play: The Psychology of Human Relationships*. New York: Penguin, 1973.

Branden, Nathaniel. *The Psychology of Self-Esteem*. New York: Bantam, 1969.

Carse, James P. *Breakfast at the Victory: The Mysticism of Ordinary Experience*. Toronto: HarperCollins Canada, 1995.

Crockett, M.J. "Restricting Temptations: Neural Mechanisms of Precommitment." *Neuron* 79, no. 2 (July 2013): 391–401.

Epstein, Mark. *Thoughts Without a Thinker*. New York: Basic Books, 1995.

Ferrucci, Piero. *What We May Be*. New York: J.P. Tarcher, 1982.

_____. *Your Inner Will: Finding Personal Strength at Critical Times*. New York: Penguin, 2014.

Ford, Debbie. *The Dark Side of the Light Chasers*. New York: Riverhead Books, 1998.

Gandhi, Mahatma. *All Men Are Brothers: Autobiographical Reflections*. Edited by Krishna Kripalani. Paris: UNESCO/Columbia University Press, 1958.

Goleman, Daniel. *Emotional Intelligence*. New York: Bantam, 1995.

Hobbes, Thomas. *Leviathan, Or The Matter, Forme & Power of a Common-Wealth Ecclesiasticall and Civill*. London, 1651.

Hoffman, Morris B. *The Punisher's Brain: The Evolution of Judge and Jury*. Cambridge, MA: Cambridge University Press, 2014.

Horn, Art. *Beyond Ego: Influential Leadership Starts Within*. Toronto: ECW, 2008.

_____. *Face It: Recognizing and Conquering the Hidden Fear That Drives All Conflict at Work.* New York: Amacom, 2004.

_____. *Gifts of Leadership: Team Building Through Focus and Empathy.* Toronto: Stoddart, 1997.

James, William. *The Principles of Psychology*, vol. 1. New York: Dover, 1950.

Kahneman, Daniel. *Thinking, Fast and Slow.* New York: Farrar, Straus and Giroux, 2011.

Kalenscher, Tobias. *Decisions in the Brain: The Role of the Avian Forebrain (Nidopallium Caudolaterale) in Decision-Making.* Sarrebrücken, Germany: VDM Verlag, 2008.

Maslow, Abraham H. *Motivation and Personality.* 2nd ed. New York: Harper & Row, 1954.

Oaten, Megan, and Ken Cheng. "Longitudinal Gains in Self-Regulation from Regular Physical Exercise." *British Journal of Health Psychology* 11, part 4 (November 2006): 717–33.

Patrick, Vanessa M., and Henrik Hagtvedt. "I Don't Versus I Can't: When Empowered Refusal Motivates Goal-Directed Behavior." *Journal of Consumer Research* 39, no. 2 (2012): 371–81.

Peck, M. Scott. *The Road Less Traveled and Beyond: Spiritual Growth in an Age of Anxiety.* New York: Simon & Schuster, 1997.

Rogers, Carl R., and Fritz J. Roethlisberger. "Barriers and Gateways to Communication." *Harvard Business Review* (November/December 1991, reprint).

Sartre, Jean-Paul. *Being and Nothingness.* New York: Washington Square Press, 1966.

Schumann, Karina. "An Affirmed Self and a Better Apology: The Effect of Self-Affirmation on Transgressors' Responses to Victims." *Journal of Experimental Social Psychology* 54 (September 2014): 89–96.

Seligman, Martin E.P. *Learned Optimism: How to Change Your Mind and Your Life.* New York: Pocket Books, 1992.

Siegel, Daniel. *Mindsight: Change Your Brain and Your Life.* New York: Random House, 2010.

Varki, Ajit, and Danny Brower. *Denial: Self-Deception, False Beliefs, and the Origins of the Human Mind.* New York: Hachette, 2013.

Wiley, Norgert. *Inner Speech and the Dialogical Self: An Unexplored Continent.* Philadelphia: Temple University Press, 2016.

INDEX

accountability
  algorithm and, 160
  challenges of, 73, 102–03, 112–13, 117, 126
  chapter on, 38–46
  culture of, 31, 39, 56, 65–67, 73, 79, 85, 110, 126–27, 139–40, 143, 146, 149, 164–70
  genuine, 68, 98, 129–30, 140, 158, 164, 170, 177
  hardball, 43, 159, 162–63, 177
  inside, 157–61, 164, 170
  institutionalizing, 163–65, 170–75
  large organizations and, 170–75
  learning initiative and, 170–75
  nurturing and, 100, 139, 144, 155, 177
  organizations and, 100, 104, 129, 157–78
  outside, 157–58, 160, 162, 170
  personal, 29, 44, 100, 112, 118, 137
  realball, 159–64, 167, 177
  self-assessment and, *140*, 141–43
  self-esteem and, 32, 44, 100, 172–73, 175
  softball, 159, 162–63, 177
  summing up, 176–78
"Anthem." *See under* Cohen, Leonard
appetites, 54, 69, 75–77, 108, 119–20, 122, 131–32
Assagioli, Roberto, 76
attention deficit disorder, 57, 113, 122

behaviour, 29–31, 44–45, 71, 75, 79, 98–99, 102–05, 109, 121, 137, 141, 154, 171, 174–75
  ethical, 79
  defensive, 93
  non-defensive, 91
  non-productive, 87
  personal, 24, 56, 152, 175
  responsible, 28, 31, 39, 53
  right, 41
  targeted, 35

blame
    apologies and, 95–98
    chapter on, 82–99
    defensiveness and, 90–93
    emotional element of, 84–85, 94
    fallacy of single cause and,
        85–86
    forgiveness and, 97–98
    freedom from, 98–99
    interdepartmental, 89–90
    polarities and, 89–90
    productive approaches instead
        of, 88–89
    reasons for, 87–88
    self-esteem and, 85
Brower, Danny
    *Denial: Self-Deception, False
        Beliefs, and the Origins of
        the Human Mind*, 54

capacity, 48, 54, 67, 77, 101, 154
career coach/coaching, 42, 46, 100–
    01, 112–13, 134, 140, 148–49,
    152–53, 171–72, 175
Cheng, Ken, 79
Cohen, Leonard
    "Anthem," 101
commitment
    algorithms of, 58–62
    backdrop factors of, 59–60
    bad faith and, 53–55
    chapter on, 47–68
    declarations of, 41
    detractors and, 59
    device(s) of, 60–61, 68, 163
    emotions and, 62

    enhancing, 65–67
    factors of, 48–49
    improvement of skills in,
        62–63
    inability to fulfill, 64–65
    intrinsic, 49–52
    leap of faith and, 52–53
    positive input and, 58–60
    procrastination and, 62
    promise breakers of, 55–58
    self-esteem and, 59, 127
    summing up, 67–68
    trouble with, 63–64
    visualization and, 60–62
Commitment Intensity Line,
    50–51, 68
communications
    companies and, 23, 25
    individual, 39, 44, 112, 120,
        165
    organizations and, 84, 90,
        100, 115
    systems and, 20, 166, 170, 173
compensation, 20, 32, 35, 41, 43, 100
confrontation, 41, 59, 69, 63, 73,
    105, 156–57
consciousness, 23, 25, 38, 45, 53–54,
    57, 61, 82, 101, 104, 134, 141,
    148, 176–78
consequences, 18, 20, 34–35, 39, 44,
    63–64, 114, 119, 157–60, 170

*Denial: Self-Deception, False Beliefs,
    and the Origins of the Human
    Mind. See under* Brower,
    Danny; Varki, Ajit

distractions, 59, 69–70, 76–81, 102, 120–21, 131, 144, 165

ego, 88, 90, 94, 122
egocentricity, 59, 110, 112
emotional intelligence, 71–72
employee
    autonomy, 44, 66, 78, 118, 146, 155, 175
    commitment, 65–68
employee performance, 65–66, 91, 100, 158, 167
    challenges, 79, 109, 116, 127–28
    monitoring and measuring, 65, 71, 74, 79, 164
    optimizing, 164, 167, 174–75
enablers/enabling, 73, 102, 112, 119–20, 122, 128, 131, 139, *140–41*, 142, 143, 148, 171

facilitators/facilitating, *140–41*, 142, 143, 171, 173
failure, 18–20, 27, 29, *36–37*, 41, 48, 59, 64, 67, 74, 86, 88, 99
feelings, 16, 27, 33, 53–54, 68, 83, 93, 95, 97, 110–12, 115, 157
    negative, 54, 57, 59–60, 84–85, 91, 126, 133, 135
    positive, 62, 64, 120, *125*, 133, 145
    strong, 58, 64, 80, 112, 150
Ferrucci, Piero, 76

Gandhi, Mahatma, 97–98
Gestalt therapy, 77

goal-oriented, 37, 156, 159–61, 175

Hobbes, Thomas
    Leviathan, 30
humanistic, 100, *141*, 143, 156–57

I Love Lucy, 7
intervention, 27, 161, 163, 171

job description, 27, 32, 66, 113, 146, 163–64
Jung, Carl, 152

label/labelling, 28, 55, 77, 81, 93, 102–03, 108, 114, 135, 165, 170
leadership, 13, 32, 66, 73, 79, 111, 139–56, 167, 173
    culture of, 155–56
    elevating people and, 148–51, 177
    group, 171
    non-judgment and, 152–55
    polarity management and, 150, *151*, 152
    self-assessment and, *140–42*, 143
    self-esteem and, 143–47
    senior, 41, 53
    skills, 79, 167, 172
    styles, 156, 161
Leviathan. See under Hobbes, Thomas

management
    organization, 19, 20, 42–44, 70, 146, 170

performance, 20, 41, 48, 167, 174

polarity, 152

responsibility, 31

self-, 147

Marathon (Ontario), 14–15

Maslow's hierarchy of needs, 120

meditation, 13, 14, 176

mental health, 48, 80, 90

mental mechanics, 100

milestones, 164

motivation, 31, 44, 51, 54, 62, 66, 75, 83, 93, 115, 116

northern Ontario, 13

Oaten, Megan, 79

objectives, 20, 35, 54, 74, 100, 115, 156, 164–69

obstacles to accountability, 22–23, 34, 41, 53, 66, 71, 100–22, 127–30, 134–35, 145, 162, 173, 175

guided reflection and, 101

humanistic, 100

initial thoughts and, *107*

is/ought dilemma and, 101, 121, 129, 132, 134

list of twelve obstacles, 101–02, 130–31

being enabled by others, 119–20, 128

compulsion to care for others, 113–14

distractions and preoccupations, 120–21

fear, 104–05, 128

feeling conflicted, 115–16, 128

feeling like a victim, 109–10, 128

hazy accountability, 102–04

imposed duties, 116–18, 128

negative self-talk, 105–09, 128

productive stances and, *107*

self-absorption, 110–12, 128

self-esteem and, 108

simple overload, 115

unhelpful conclusions and, *107*

wiring, 112–13, 128

Odysseus, 72

optimism, 33, 59, 89

ownership, 21–23, 27, 31–34, 38, 45, 114, 149, 162, 165

Peck, M. Scott
The Road Less Traveled and Beyond, 80

performance, 41, 42, 66, 71, 100, 116, 158, 164

indicators, 79, 100, 143, 174

monitoring and measuring of, 3, 65, 74, 79, 100, 164

optimizing, 164–67, 175

organization, 40, 41, 109

poor, 35, 45, 79, 127

review, 55, 79, 91, 143, 174

systems, 48, 174

personnel
   operations, 89, 116, 150
   service, 73, 117–18
preoccupations, 59, 102, 107,
   120–21
procrastination, 25, 60, 62, 69,
   71, 74, 115, *125*, 127, 128,
   136
psychological
   needs, 147
   obstacle, 41
   strategy, 100
   threat, 44, 143–44
   well-being, 143
   withdrawal, 109
psychologists, 48, 74, 76, 86, 105
psychology, 71, 176
   accountability, 38
   commitment, 49
psychotherapy, 64, 176

reflection, 100–01
   self-, 37, 103
research, 48, 72–74, 97
respect, 59, 63, 78, 160
   disrespect, 111
   self-, 32, 59, 94, 127
responsibility, 18–25, *35*, 42–47, 83,
   88, 96–97, 103, 118, *124–26*,
   127–28, 132, 139, 155, 175–
   78
   chapter on, 27–37
   corporate, 30, 32
   definition of, 28–29
   fear of, 59
   ideas of, 27

irresponsibility, 41, 57, 106,
   115, 119, 130
nurturing, 36, 68
obstacles to, 113, 116–17, 119
personal, 18, 22, 26, 35–37,
   45, 68, 73, 79, 90, 95, 99,
   114, 139, 142–44, 150,
   160, 163–64, 170–77
phases of, 76–78
self-, 22, 33, 34–37, 42, 45,
   67, 88, 91–92, 95–96,
   99, 106, 116–17, *125–27*,
   160, 170
self-assessment of, *36–37*
self-esteem and, 143–47, 159
types of, 35
The Road Less Traveled and Beyond.
   See under Peck, M. Scott

Sartre, Jean-Paul, 54
satisfaction
   job, 100–01, 118, 127, 165,
   172, 174
   life, 62, 100, 101, 123, 178
self-acceptance/self-accountability,
   26, 37, 59, 71, 92, 122, 131–33,
   141–43, 157, 158
self-assessment, 37, *123–27*, 133,
   139, *140–42*
self-coaching
   baby steps for change, *136–37*
   chapter on, 123–38
   choosing a soft spot, 133–34
   committing to change, 137–38
   common outcomes, 127–28
   identifying the obstacle, 134–35

"Prime Directive," 129–31
process of, 133–38
results of, 128–29
survey, *124–26*
website documents, 123, 138
self-deception, 54, 67
self-esteem, 71, 79, 127
aggression and anger and, 44
definition of, 78
healthy, 32, 44, 59, 70, 78
low, 78–79, 85, 143, 144
strategies for, 70, 75, 79–81,
100, 143
self-nurturing, 113, 126, 128
stress, 48, 76, 95–97, 120, 135
systems
organizational, 19, 20–21,
35–37, 48, 66, 79, 90,
113, 139, 164, 174
personal, 112, 113

temptation, 27, 28, 52, 70–80,
175
Thoreau, Henry David
Walden; or, Life in the Woods,
60–61
Thunder Bay (Ontario), 14
transactional analysis theory, 94

Varki, Ajit
*Denial: Self-Deception, False
Beliefs, and the Origins of
the Human Mind*, 54
visualization, 50, 60–61, 68, 71,
118, 120, 171
vulnerability, 59, 95, 130

*Walden; or, Life in the Woods. See
under* Thoreau, Henry David
West Point (New York), 17–20, 37,
126
willpower, 16, 20, 21, 27, 48, 59,
100–01, 127–30, 144–45, 178
appetites and, 75–77
chapter on, 69–81
commitment devices and,
72–73
definition of, 70–71
experiencing, 75
less, 78
more, 69, 71, 73, 78, 133
procrastination and, 71
self-esteem and, 44, 70–72, 75,
78–81, 127
sense of, 44
source of, 71, 75
tricks of trade and, 73–75

dundurn.com   dundurnpress

@dundurnpress   dundurnpress

dundurnpress   info@dundurn.com

FIND US ON NETGALLEY & GOODREADS TOO!

DUNDURN